POLAND INTO THE 1990s

POLAND INTO THE 1990s

Economy and Society in Transition

EDITED BY
GEORGE BLAZYCA AND *RYSZARD RAPACKI*

Pinter Publishers
London

© The editors and contributors, 1991

First published in Great Britain in 1991 by
Pinter Publishers, 25 Floral Street, London WC2E 9DS

All rights reserved. No part of this publication may be reproduced, stored in a retrieval system, or transmitted by any other means without the prior permission of the copyright holder. Please direct all enquiries to the publishers.

British Library Cataloguing in Publication Data
A CIP catalogue record for this book is available from the British Library

ISBN 0 86187 134 0

Typeset by Florencetype Ltd and
Printed and bound in Great Britain
by Biddles Ltd.

CONTENTS

List of figures	vi
List of tables	vii
Notes on contributors	ix
Introduction: Poland into the 1990s *George Blazyca and Ryszard Rapacki*	1
1 Polish society after the communist experiment *Edmund Wnuk-Lipiński*	4
2 Poland's political system – change and future scenarios *Kazimierz Kloc*	11
3 Poland: systemic reforms and economic policy in the 1990s *Dariusz K. Rosati*	20
4 Environment *Michal Rusiński*	32
5 Energy and conservation *Marek Lubiński*	44
6 Agriculture *Andrzej Kowalski*	56
7 Housing *Jacek Łaszek*	63
8 Capital investments *Andrzej Parkoła*	73
9 Prices, incomes and the consumer market *Marian Górski*	84
10 The banking system and monetary policy *Grzegorz T. Jędrzejczak and Krzysztof Kalicki*	95
11 Privatisation and the private sector *Grzegorz T. Jędrzejczak*	107
12 External disequilibrium and adjustment processes *Krzysztof Kalicki*	118
13 Foreign trade *Ryszard Rapacki*	135
Index	147

List of figures

9.1	Disequilibrium on consumer market 1978–88	88
12.1	Import/Net Material Product 1980–8	121
12.2	Export/Net Material Product 1980–8	122
12.3	Current account balance 1980–8	123
12.4	Trade balance 1980–8	124
12.5	Debt in Transferable Roubles and dollars 1980–8	129
12.6	Debt/export 1980–8	130
12.7	Interest/export 1980–8	131

List of tables

3.1	The economy 1981–8	24
5.1	The fuel and energy balance 1975–90	45
5.2	Energy indicators for the national economy 1963–87	49
7.1	Housing density	66
7.2	The housing situation 1988	67
7.3	Investor structure in housing construction 1952–88	68
8.1	Capital investment 1982	74
8.2	Capital investment in the socialized industrial sector 1982	75
8.3	Capital investment outlays 1978, 1982 and 1988	76
8.4	Investment outlays in socialized industry 1978, 1982 and 1987	77
8.5	Investment growth 1983–8	78
8.6	Investment 1988	79
8.7	Investment in state industry 1987	79
8.8	Abandoned investments in the state sector 1983–7	81
9.1	Disequilibrium on the consumer market 1978–88	87
10.1	Companies with zero credit rating 1987–8	102
10.2	Changes illustrating monetary policy 1982–9	103
10.3	Changes illustrating monetary policy 1989–90	105
11.1	Public and private ownership 1988	108
11.2	Firms and average employment 1988	109
11.3	Distribution of public enterprises in industry 1988	109
11.4	State- and privately-owned agriculture 1988	110
11.5	Firms and employment in construction 1988	111
11.6	Services rendered for households 1988	111
12.1	Imports on credit terms 1981–8	119
12.2	Inflow of new loans 1980–9	119
12.3	Variables in foreign trade 1980–9	125
12.4	Hard currency maturity payments 1982–9	126
12.5	Official debt rescheduling 1981–90	127
12.6	Rescheduling private banks' loans 1981–8	127

12.7	Indebtedness 1980–9	128
12.8	The financial situation 1980–9	130
12.9	Expected debt service 1989–98	132
13.1	Poland in a world and European context 1978–88	135
13.2	GMP, exports and imports 1980–8	137
13.3	Growth of exports and imports 1980–8	138
13.4	Foreign trade balance 1981–8	140
13.5	Commodity structure of exports 1985–8	141
13.6	Terms of trade 1980–8	142
13.7	End-use composition of imports 1980–8	142

Notes on contributors

George Blazyca Acting Head of the School of Social Sciences at Thames Polytechnic in London, teaches Economics and is a leading UK commentator on Polish economic affairs.

Ryszard Rapacki, Associate Professor of Economics and Head of the Department of Economics in the Foreign Trade Faculty at the Central School of Planning and Statistics (SGPiS) in Warsaw. His main research interests include international technology transfer, multinational enterprise, export promotion and trade policies, systemic reforms in Eastern Europe, economic development and investment appraisal, acts as consultant to a number of organizations including UNIDO.

Marian Górski is an Associate Professor at Warsaw University and specialises in macroeconomics. Since 1989 he has acted also as a consultant to the Ministry of Finance.

Grzegorz T. Jędrzejczak is an Associate Professor in the Management Faculty of Warsaw University. His main interests lie in financial and monetary regulation and its impact on business. He is an advisor in the government's 'Privatization Office' and co-author of the privatization programme. At present he is chairman of a government group preparing capital market regulations.

Krzysztof Kalicki teaches international finance in the Foreign Trade Faculty at SGPiS and is a consultant to the National Bank. His main research interests include monetary theory and policy, monetary theory of exchange rates and balance of payments, exchange rate forecasting and international and corporate finance.

Kazimierz Kloc teaches Political Science at SGPiS and is an advisor to the Ministry of Employment.

Andrzej Kowalski teaches Economics in the Department of Agricultural Economics at Warsaw's SGPiS. His research interests include land economics and social policy in agriculture.

Jacek Łaszek teaches Economics at Warsaw's SGPiS, has special interests in housing and social policy.

Marek Lubiński, Associate Professor in the Foreign Trade Faculty at SGPiS, and deputy dean of the Faculty since 1985, his main research interests are business cycles, environmental and energy problems.

Andrej Parkoła teaches Economics in the Foreign Trade Faculty at SGPiS. His main research interests include national economic management, structural change in the economy and exports promotion policy.

Dariusz Rosati is Director of the Foreign Trade Research Institute in Warsaw and Associate Professor of Economics in the Foreign Trade Faculty at SGPiS. Has acted as a consultant to many commercial and international organizations including Citibank, UNIDO and the ILO. Main research interests include forecasting, foreign trade policy, investment appraisal, systemic reforms in planned economies, inflation and development economics.

Michal Rusiński works for the Foreign Trade Ministry, dealing with international economic organizations, and teaches Economics at SGPiS. Major research interests include West European integration, environmental – economic interrelationships and industrial policy.

Edmund Wnuk-Lipiński is Associate Professor of Sociology at the Institute of Philosophy and Sociology of the Polish Academy of Sciences where he heads research into social inequality. He also heads the team of sociological advisers to Solidarity Members of Parliament and was a member of the Solidarity team involved in the February to March 1989 Round Table talks with the government.

♦ INTRODUCTION ♦
Poland into the 1990s

George Blazyca and Ryszard Rapacki

For communist leaderships in Eastern Europe it must have seemed, in 1989, that the sky was falling in. At the start of the year the big changes were taking place in Poland with the remarkable (and unthinkable just a few months earlier) Round Table discussions between authorities and opposition. But the even more astonishing thing about the Round Table is that to the end, right up to April 1989, the ruling group, the Party, was determined to stay in charge. It intended no more than to allow the opposition a limited participation in a forthcoming general election and the formula was precise: a 35% slice of parliamentary seats. For the Polish Party, the limits on the pace and scale of democratization were clear and firm.

But history did not follow the Party's pre-set rules and in September 1989 it was Tadeusz Mazowiecki who sat in the Council of Ministers office as head of a coalition government in which Solidarity played the leading role. The Polish pace of political development was extraordinarily rapid, but even this was soon to be overtaken, when the most momentous of all the 1989 changes took place when the Berlin Wall came crashing down on 9 November. As Neal Ascherson put it in the *Independent* the next day,

> It wasn't just the landscape of European politics that suddenly changed last night. It was the European cosmos. For most west Europeans now alive, the world has always ended at the East German border and the Wall: beyond lay darkness and demons. The opening of the frontiers declares that the world has no edge any more. Europe is becoming once more round and whole.

The idea behind this book is to bring together, from a former principality in the land of 'darkness and demons', some current thinking on key social, political and economic issues. We commissioned special papers from leading social scientists on some of the critical issues facing Poland as it tries to make the leap from 'actually existing socialism' to Western-style capitalism. The contributors are all Polish citizens (with the exception of one co-editor), living in Poland and with a commitment to the economic and political reconstruction of the country. Indeed, many of our authors are associated, in one way or another, with Solidarity or, in an advisory capacity, with the Mazowiecki government.

At the time of writing, in late July 1990, Poland had gone through a difficult half year, under a fiercely tight monetary squeeze, designed to bring a hyperinflation under control. It appeared to work: a monthly inflation rate of almost 30% in the second half of 1989 was brought down, after a temporary upward 'blip' in January 1990, to only 3.4% in June. But the cost was immense, real incomes were cut by around 36% in the first half of 1990 (compared to the same 1989 period), output fell by 30% and unemployment accelerated sharply upwards (from next to nothing in December 1989 to over half a million, or 3.8% of the non-agricultural labour force, in June 1990). There were signs too of a growing social restiveness as railway workers threatened a national strike (in May 1990) and farmers blocked main roads in protest at expensive credit, low prices and falling demand (in June/July). Opinion polls suggested that though the government's popularity remained impressively solid it was none the less slowly being dented by the incessant assault on living standards. On reviewing the first half year results the authorities decided that the time was right to make crucial adjustments to policy to try to switch the economy more decisively towards recovery.

By the middle of 1990 it was becoming generally agreed that the Balcerowicz plan in its 'Mark 1' shape was too severe on domestice demand. As many in Poland put it, it was like 'shooting a sparrow with too many cannon'. If firms faced, as subsidies were removed, 'hard budget constraints', as well as positive real interest rates then perhaps it was not necessary so tightly to keep a lid on wages growth via a highly restrictive tax based incomes policy. If the złoty was steeply devalued (by 32% overnight at the start of 1990) then perhaps the steep import duties which were also imposed contributed to 'over-kill' on the demand side. All of this argued for some easing of the tightness of the demand deflation. But the argument was supplemented by a supply-side factor too. Enterprises had stubbornly refused to adapt to the new demand situation in the way that the authorities had hoped. Instead of looking for new markets and cost cutting through greater efficiency, firms responded to the 'demand barrier' in what for them was the easiest way. It was summed up by one Polish writer in the following manner,

> Can't find sales – then limit production and send workers on holiday. Still trouble, substitute unpaid for paid leave . . . Then it's necessary to lose a few people. If the market still doesn't want our goods then instead of reducing prices or exporting we again cut production, let the next group of workers go, and so on. In this way the enterprise can die standing up so long as there is a solitary director in the plant to turn the lights off.[1]

Some observers also pointed to another failing of the programme – it was not addressed in any clear manner to any particular social group or groups. This meant that it did not call on the active support of anyone though it relied crucially on the passive support of all. But perhaps in Polish conditions this is not enough particularly when it is nothing less than an entire system transformation that is proposed?

None of this should be taken to suggest that 'Balcerowicz Mark 1' was unsuccessful. Inflation *was* brought down, firms came up against hard budget constraints for the first time (something that had evaded previous economic reformers for at least twenty years), the socially insidious złoty black market was eliminated and that other Polish phenomenon, universal shortage, disappeared as rationing by queue and 'who-knows-who' was replaced by rationing by price and income.

But the next steps in the 'transformation programme' are more fundamental and may be more trying. Poland will need to overcome the legacy of forty years of generally misconceived economic policy. Post-communist governments will need to deal with an immense economic restructuring as each country seeks to find some area of comparative advantage. What seems clear is that it will not be, in Poland's case, in coal, steel or ships. It may be in agri-business and food processing but this is likely to require an agrarian transformation (in the already private agriculture) that will be every bit as traumatic and long-term as privatization in the state sector. It may be in tourism though this will require a massive clean up of coast, rivers and air – resources scandalously squandered over the past forty years. And no doubt there will be other sectors where highly skilled, adaptable and relatively cheap labour will find openings. The indigenous private sector is notoriously under-developed, was deliberately neglected in the past, but must also have great potential for the future.

It is clear that Poland, like other post-communist economies, has huge investment needs, for restructuring and industrial modernization, for the business infrastructure in finance and banking, for cleaning-up and making safe the environment, for housing and for health. Without considerable capital inflow it is hard to see how the transformation to Western-style economy can succeed. This means too that the $40 bn Polish debt is surely as good as written off. There is no real possibility of it being repaid and even to insist on servicing a portion of it, as was the case during the 1980s, seems pointless now.

Undoubtedly, difficult times lie ahead as Poland moves into the 1990s and there is a residual danger that, if the going gets too tough, the unemployment too high and for too long, and the degree of Western assistance is too parsimonious, the country could slip backwards towards a strong-arm internal politics of an almost pre-war vintage. It would be a tragedy if the democratization that has been the Solidarity emblem since 1980 were to be swamped by a misplaced romanticism for a bygone age.

Notes

1. Bacyński, 'Prepraszam, może pomóc? (Excuse me, can I help?), *Pólityka*, 7 April 1990.

CHAPTER 1

Polish society after the communist experiment

Edmund Wnuk-Lipiński

1. Introduction

Since 1989 Europe has been larger; the Eastern Block countries are undergoing a profound transition from communist system to.... Yes, it is a good question to what? What is the direction of the peaceful revolutions in Poland, Hungary, Czechoslovakia, Bulgaria, and – of course – the Soviet Union? What about the bloody revolution in Romania; was it inevitable or could it also have taken the path of radical, but peaceful transformation? Will the changes taking place in Eastern Europe continue to be peaceful? Do they have any common denominator? And if so, can any social theory explain the social and political mechanisms now at work throughout the region?

The aim of this chapter is to suggest a way of understanding the processes we are witnessing in Eastern Europe, and particulary in Poland, for the Polish case seems to be an especially good example of the broader trends occurring in previously communist society.

To understand recent developments one has to recall earlier social and political transformations. The first and the most basic was completed by the early 1950s and is often labelled the 'Stalinist period'. During Stalinism Poland was also transformed from a traditional to a mass society. But it was also a monocentric society, one that, as Ossowski[1] has put it, could be understood in the theoretical framework of 'totalitarianism' developed by Friedrich and Brzezinski, Arendt, Kornhauser and others.[2]

In Poland the totalitarian system was implemented only in a 'distorted' manner. Even when Stalinism was at its peak the Catholic Church retained its separate and distinctive place in society and independent rural communities remained relatively strong. The forced collectivization of agriculture failed to destroy the basic social bonds in villages, bonds also supported and nurtured by the Church. Polish society has shown a very low tolerance for the system change which was brought about by the victorious Red Army at the end of the Second World War.

Today, society is in the delicate process of passing from one system to another. The process is so fragile because it has taken the form of a new type of revolution, a non-violent restoration of 'normality' in economic, social and political life. But to explain this process more fully it is necessary to indicate what kind of institutional, structural and cultural changes were imposed by the communist regime, and to what extent the changes were subsequently rejected or absorbed by society.

2. The single-centre–monoparty system

The monocentric order was built in Poland step by step. Immediately after the Second World War the communists took power under the umbrella of the Red Army; the late 1940s were the years of struggle for total dominance over the political life of the country. Totalitarian power structures were completely in place by 1948, when opposition was finally eliminated from public life and the Communist Party remained alone on the public political scene.

At the same time a profound economic transformation took place. State property grew in importance while private property was almost eliminated. The process started in heavy industry but soon spread elsewhere to other branches of industry, to services and to trade. It was accompanied by land reform and a parallel concentration of state ownership of land. This was facilitated by the fact that vast areas of what had been eastern Poland were transferred to the USSR, and territorial compensation in the West fell mainly into the hands of the state.

During that period agricultural policy seemed to be inconsistent; on the one hand the authorities wanted total control over agricultural production and the quickest way to achieve that was through land ownership. On the other hand, however, the new regime needed social support, at least in the first stage of the construction of a monocentric order. And land reform had, first of all, a political goal: to win some measure of support in the countryside. But is was only a temporary solution. In fact, the strategic goal (concentration of all land under the control of the central power) was accomplished in the early 1950s, when forced collectivization reached its zenith. From that moment market mechanisms ceased to regulate a major part of the Polish economy.

In the meantime, there were equally profound transformations in the social sphere. Only the Catholic Church succeeded in preserving its independence (though this was quite limited at that time), all other social institutions (political parties, voluntary organizations, local community associations, youth organizations and professional assocations) were destroyed or controlled by the central power. In that way social relations functioned almost exclusively via the formal network of institutions subordinated to the centre. In effect, there was a growing social isolation and atomization of groups and individuals.

In that peculiar period of the early 1950s Polish society came closest to the ideal type of the monocentric system whose characteristic features are:
  – central control over organizations,
  – blocking of any autonomous social dynamic (normally activated by market rules) resulting in an atrophy of class structure,
  – social isolation of smaller groups (due to the ban on voluntary associations

created independently of the centre),
- emergence of the second economy (a result of the inevitable incompleteness of central planning).

In short, a monocentric order exists where one central authority organizes collective life in line with its own principles and values (which are not necessarily shared by the majority of the population).

In Poland this period did not last long. After the 1956 crisis, private farmers got their land back, and from that moment the system began to change. However, some of its essential features survived until 1989. The system certainly outlived its internal potential and this is probably the most important cause of the prolonged economic and social crisis experienced by Polish society.

3. Institutions

In an ideal type of monocentric order there is no room for independent institutions in public life. The whole organizational structure of a society is hierarchical, centralized and subordinated to one power centre. This general principle is applied in political life (the single party), economy (central planning), and in social life (hierarchical social and cultural organizations). The state becomes the only medium of social relations, and institutionalized social relations are – as Narojek[3] has put it – state-owned. In such circumstances the system may survive, for a time, even without social support.

In Poland in the late 1940s the communist regime eliminated political opposition as the first step in its quest for total control over society. Surviving social institutions had to transform themselves. Trade unions became 'transmission belts' for Party decisions instead of being an organized defence of workers' interests; youth organizations ceased to be associations of those sharing similar values, political beliefs or life-style and were fused into huge, mass institutions with almost compulsory membership, whose basic function became ideological indoctrination.

Thus, in the early 1950s public life in Poland was, with the exception of the Church, filled by institutions 'created from above'. The institutional changes needed to support a stable monocentric order were complete.

4. Social structure

The impact of all of this on Polish society was great. It led to an atrophy of the class structure which had been formed between the two world wars. Poland's new political system socially levelled the population. All the means of production came under state ownership, but property rights were unclear and – in a way - anonymous. Every organization active in public life was either subordinated to the centre's control or disbanded and replaced. Public organizations became instruments for carrying out executive decisions rather than for the projection of social forces. Even the Church struggled hard to preserve what was left of its autonomy; its influence in public life having been reduced to a minimum. At the same time, the removal of landowners from their land and its subsequent distribution put an end to the country's landed gentry; the nationalization of industry resulted in the disappearance of the bourgeoisie, whereas the middle class perished in the 'battle for commerce', as the then official propaganda called the nationalization of trade and services.

The atrophy of the former class structure and loss of any market-generated dynamism led to a situation in which a new type of social dynamic had to be created and applied, namely a mobilization of the masses, imposed from the top and focused on carrying out tasks set by the centre as well as keeping the people occupied. Mobilization became an essential tool in integrating the masses around centralized organizational structures. It was much later, especially in the 1970s, that centrally generated mobilization gradually gave way to widespread corruption.

The monocentric 'macro' order had a major impact on the shape and functioning of 'micro' structures. While individual social groups and organizations were deliberately fragmented and atomized, informal structures soon began to appear within formal organizations. Rychard[4] observed that at a certain point the authorities began to perceive society as a 'hostile environment'. And of course the centralized organizational order was certainly a 'hostile environment' as far as small groups were concerned. But within formal organizations, micro structures soon emerged and provided a forum for a behind-closed-doors articulation and mediation of interests. At the same time small groups outside formal structures (families, circles of friends, small local communities) succeeded in preserving those values which were absent in society's highly formalized and ritualized public life.

5. Values

Poland has been a Christian nation for over one thousand years and the values of Western civilization are deeply rooted in Polish culture. The new social order, implemented in Poland after the Second World War, brought an alternative, and often contradictory, set of values. A clash of the two value systems was inevitable.

The institutions controlled by the centre filled almost the entire public space and anyone entering the public arena had to accept the centre's rules. Those rules were built on values quite different from the native cultural tradition (the new rules insisted on the dominance of the collective over the individual; the depreciation of individual freedom, of private property and of religious beliefs). None the less a complex network of informal micro structures came into being which sheltered traditional values. There was room in the family and within small groups of friends for the inter-generational transmission of traditional values displaced by public life in the communist period.

This process, however, brought a sharp split – a 'social dimorphism' – between the public and private spheres of life.[5] A duality of social life has been observed in highly diverse societies ranging from the 'primitive' to the modern. But in monocentric social order this phenomenon is particularly strong, and – in a way – it is one of the factors stablizing the whole system.

The monocentric communist system organized collective life in Poland for over four decades. Most members of society have lived under this system from birth and, until recently, had no experience of pluralistic social life. The first emergence of Solidarity in public life in 1980 was too short for a significant reconstruction of institutions in politics, economy or society. But this period brought – on a mass scale – an experience which was to prove very important in the years to come. It ended social isolation and atomization. A rich collective life beyond the scope of formal institutions emerged. Independent cultural and political activities came into being alongside the already independent (if frequently corrupt) second economy. The emergence of Solidarity considerably reduced 'social dimorphism' but martial law restored it. Nevertherless the experience of 1980–1 was memorized in social consciousness and stimulated further transformations which are by no means over. Moreover, it hardly needs to be mentioned that change today, at the start of the 1990s, has a greater momentum because it is not limited to one isolated country but is a feature of the region as a whole.

6. Comments on the recent upheavals

It is clear that the recent changes in Eastern Europe must be considered in terms of a social process rather than an act. It is utopian to believe that the monocentric order, which was constructed and working for decades, may be removed overnight. Deep change requires a reconstruction of institutions, the emergence of new elites, the organization of new social forces which will assure the stability of a new social order, and – last but not least – revolution in social consciousness. Bearing all this in mind one may say that most Eastern Europe societies had a honeymoon in late 1989 or early 1990 and serious economic and political problems will come when revolutionary euphoria disappears.

Polish society experienced its honeymoon period in 1980–1, and solid foundations for a polycentric order are now being built; both political and economic. In politics there is a shift from the monoparty infrastructure to multiparty political life. In the economy there is a shift from a logic of concentration of all resources in state agencies which are governed by one political force, to market-type regulation of economic relations. This may not be spectacular but it is crucial for the stability of the new order. And when profound reconstruction involves an entire economy then the process meets formidable obstacles, for it threatens the vital interests of various social groups. The long existence of a monocentric order created a network of interests which are threatened by the transition from non-market to market economy. A new economic order will certainly destroy vested economic interests, and before a network of new interests emerges there will be a difficult transitional period when the old system ceases to work and the new one does not work to its full capacity.

Since 1989, a formerly clear configuration of social forces (communist power versus democratic opposition, supported by the majority of society) has become more complex. The Communist Party was totally defeated in the June 1989 general elections and the former opposition took power. But the old apparatus of the army, security forces and administration survived. The Communist Party formally ceased to exist at the beginning of 1990, but again communist structures (in politics and economy) outlive the existence of the Party. It is true that restoration of the market mechanism will lead to a gradual erosion of those structures, but they have their own inertia. A growing tension was bound to emerge between the old institutional set up and the new social and political forces.

At the same time, there is a parallel process within the former opposition; the weaker the threat from the old regime, the more visible Solidarity's internal divisions become. Moral protest against old and worn out structures is gradually replaced by a normal political process involving the definition and mediation of group interests.

The balance of political forces in late 1989 and 1990 was shaped by the Round Table accords of early 1989. But change, since the Round Table, has been sweeping: Solidarity has won a stunning general election victory (June 1989) and, in January 1990, the Communist Party formally ceased to exist. In effect, the Round Table agreement is more and more anachronistic and does not reflect the real balance of power; this very fact became during 1990 a new source of social and political tensions. It is also important to note that large segments of society are outside any organized political group. The political behaviour of this 'silent majority' in any eventual conflict is an unknown both for politicians and social scientists. Much depends on a successful economic recovery. If the Mazowiecki–Balcerowicz economic programme succeeds, the silent majority may generate a new middle class and a stable social base for a democratic order. If, however, the economy collapses then the 'uncommitted' may support a more destructive political movement, which will postpone the Polish return to Europe. Replacement of one social order by another is always full of tensions, but examples of peaceful transition do exist (Spain is perhaps the best example).

Poland entered a critical period of transformation at the beginning of 1990. If this passage is to be concluded without any major social unrest, and especially if such eventual unrest is not transferred into a wide populist movement, then the transition from the monocentric order of a communist type to the democratic order of Western type will be successful. Otherwise this fragile yet crucial historical phase may end in another type of monocentric order, this time with a right-wing character.

Notes

1. See S. Ossowski, *Dziela* (Works), Vol. IV, PWN, Warwaw, 1967.
2. See H. Arendt, *Origins of Totalitarianism*, New Edition, New York, 1966;

C. J. Friedrich, Z. K. Brzezinski, *Totalitarian Dictatorship and Autocracy*, New York, 1956; W. Kornhauser, *The Politics of Mass Society*, Glencoe, 1959.
3. See W. Narojek, 'Perspektywy pluralizmu w upaństwowionym społeczenstwie' (The future of pluralism in an Etatist society), mimeo., Warsaw, 1984.
4. See A. Rychard, 'Władza i gospodarka – trzy perspektywy teoretyczne' (Power and the economy – three theoretical perspectives), in W. Morawski, ed., *Demokracja i gospodarka* (Democracy and economy), Warsaw, 1983.
5. See E. Wnuk-Lipiński, 'Social dimorphism and its implications' in *Crisis and Transition: Polish Society in the 1980s*, eds. I. Białecki, J. Koralewicz and M. Watson, Berg Publishers, London, 1987.

♦ CHAPTER 2 ♦

Poland's political system – change and future scenarios

Kazimierz Kloc

1. The totalitarian model – essence and evolution

The totalitarian model, of which Poland has some experience, concentrated power in the hands of the Communist Party apparatus. The state administration, the army, police, security services and the judicial system were all subordinated to it. The relative importance of each of these elements varied throughout our postwar history.[1]

The preservation of this political rule had to be based on economic control. This was achieved through nationalization and central planning. The monopoly of power in the political and economic sphere called for the establishment of control over the press, radio and TV. Social activities in various forms were also organized by the authorities. They monitored and guided the trade unions, youth organizations, and other associations.

A state dominated by a party founded on revolutionary ideology treats all the institutions of power and legal norms as instruments which can be changed at will. No rules of political life are lasting. The ruling elite makes the law and changes it as needs be. It makes law and yet, itself, remains outside its control.

The operation of political parties, Parliament and government is quite different from their Western counterparts; democratic only in name, they are a facade for real decision-making power.

There were three legal parties in Poland in the years 1949–89: the Polish United Workers' Party (PZPR – Polska Zjednoczona Partia Robotnicza), the United Peasants' Party (ZSL – Zjednoczone Stronnictwo Ludowe) and the Democratic Party (SD – Stronnictwo Demokratyczne). However, none strictly speaking, was a political party.

Real political parties compete for power and represent the specific interests of defined social groups. The Polish United Workers' Party defended a 'national interest' as defined by its apparatchiks. It was by no means a permanent representative of any significant social group. The other two parties did not participate in any real competition for power nor, in fact, were they even labelled 'parties'[2] and they accepted the 'leading role of the Polish United Workers' Party'. Their senior partner, the PZPR, even set limits on the number of their members. Their formal role was to represent rural communities, and small-time entrepreneurs plus a part of the intelligentsia. They had a number of seats reserved in Parliament and, from 1956, several less important posts in the government.

Alongside the three parties there were also the legal Catholic associations (PAX, Więź, ChSS).

Parties, associations, and other social organisations came together in the so-called Front of National Unity, a form of coalition, but really not more than a puppet of the PZPR. The visible part of its role was to put forward lists of candidates in parliamentary elections.

Parliamentary seats were shared out well in advance of any election. The majority (52% to 64%) was always reserved for the PZPR, the Peasants' Party usually had 21% to 25%, while the Democratic Party normally got between 6% and 8% of all seats. Around 10% of parliamentary space was earmarked for so-called 'non-party' MPs (including Catholic associations). Elections were in fact a sort of plebiscite designed to demonstrate support for the programme of one party. Nor were the plebiscites voluntary: people were pressured to participate.

Parliament, elected for the past forty years in accordance with principles similar to those above, did not play a major role in governing Poland. It tended to become more active only in periods of political crisis, as was the case in the years 1956–7 and 1980–1. A smaller body elected by the Parliament, the so-called Council of State, was empowered to pass decrees equal in rank to parliamentary Acts. Parliament usually rubber-stamped all of the government's and the Council of State's legislative projects and most of the time voting was unanimous.

Parliament had a negligible influence on the composition of the government and there is no record of it ever rebuking a minister for poor performance of duties.

Much governmental activity focused on economic management. However, the government did not make policy: rather its role was confined to implementing decisions made by the Central Committee of the Polish United Workers' Party. Those who held the most important government posts (prime minister, heads of the Planning Commission, the Ministry of the Interior, the Army) were also members of the highest party body (Politburo) or at least of the Central Committee.

The lack of fundamental democratic principles in the party's operation enhanced the role of professional apparatchiks. At all levels, in the central and local state and in factories, party secretaries were the politically most important people, the key decision-makers in a highly hierarchical and centralized apparatus.

But of course diverse industrial and regional interests continued to exist beneath the formally centralized rule of the party apparatus. Various groups at different levels tried to consolidate their respective positions by securing as much centrally distributed funding as possible (industrialised areas at the expense of less developed regions, industry at the expense of agriculture, police, state security and the military at the expense of education and medical services).

This permanent though hidden power struggle was confined to the apparatus. The social and political activities of the individual were channelled only within institutions created and controlled by the party. Attempts to create social organisations, associations or political parties, outside this framework were treated as a threat to the system as a whole. Society was incapacitated.

2. The Polish road from communism

Communist rule in Poland went through repressive and liberal phases. Political relaxation usually followed workers' protests against low living standards or against price increases. At such moments power struggles between factions in the ruling elite often also surfaced. Leadership changes frequently followed alongside shifts in economic policy (usually with higher consumption and curtailment of investments), economic reforms (usually combining central planning with a dose of market regulation) and of limited democratization.

In political matters it was sometimes demanded that Parliament should become a place where law *is* made, that the government *should* govern, while the PZPR should limit itself to a guiding role through its representatives in Parliament and in government. The question of the democratization of inner Party life was also frequently raised. Reformers within the Party believed that democratic elections in the Party itself would lead to a more democratic operation of the state as a whole.

Up until the early 1970s there was faith that such reform was possible. But experience showed that reforms were always abandoned two or three years after having been first announced, with the political system reverting to its earlier form. None the less the area of public life no longer fully controlled by the authorities – the social space – did slowly expand.

Looking back for example to the political turmoil of 1956 is instructive. This had three major effects. First it halted the collectivization of agriculture and resulted in the dissolution of some 90% of forcibly created agricultural cooperatives. Private land ownership and small-scale private farming was rescued and the marginal sector of private small-scale manufacturing and services also expanded. But although it survived, the private sector was surrounded by 'unfriendly' state policies, (including compulsory quotas, fixed purchase prices, high taxation) which blocked its development.

Second, the Catholic Church won major concessions. The authorities could no longer use mass reprisals against the clergy nor pressure the faithful to conceal their faith. The Church gained the right to teach religion and publish (though with some restrictions) its weekly and monthly magazines – the state's monopoly on the media was broken. New Catholic associations (Więź, Znak, ChSS) with limited parliamentary representation came into being.

Not all of the gains won by the Church proved durable however. Propaganda campaigns and police reprisals, aimed at curbing the Church's wider influence and at intimidating the clergy, were especially strong in the 1960s. None the less, neither the scale nor the methods of these operations matched those of the years 1950–6.

The third major effect of liberalization was greater freedom with regard to travel to the West. This offered a chance to learn (often facilitated through family contacts) about other political systems and had a further impact on a relative flowering of culture, literature and scientific research in Poland.

These changes weakened communist rule and created the opening that became labelled 'the Polish road to socialism'. But the concessions won from the state did not threaten it in the short term, especially since they could always be restricted. Moreover the core of the ruling system remained unchanged.

When economic and political reforms came to nothing faith in democratization of the system from within also evaporated. This lead to new forms of social behaviour, initially confined to small groups of the intelligentsia which aimed essentially to defend a certain autonomy and independence from the authorities. Independence was the rallying cry of the opposition which emerged in the 1970s. Protest letters were written against constitutional amendments which inscribed 'the leading role of the party' and 'friendship with the Soviet Union' into the constitution. The Workers Defence Committee (Komitet Obrony Robotników) organised material and legal aid for workers persecuted in connection with the 1976 prices protest. Associations were set up to defend civil rights, along with the so-called 'flying universities' and free trade unions. Efforts were made to publish periodicals and books outside the official system and its censorship. Naturally, there was a constant and consistent effort on the part of the authorities to suppress these activities.

In 1980 a generalized workers' protest swept the country and led to the birth of the first non-religious mass organization in a communist country independent of both the state and the Party. Solidarity quickly metamorphosed itself into a social movement in open opposition to the ruling system. In the early period of its legalised existence, the authorities pressured Solidarity to respect the ruling political system. Among other things, this was to consist in the acceptance of the leading role of the Polish United Workers' Party and also in abandoning all activities other than traditional trade union functions. Attempts were made to channel the new union into the old structures.

Soon trade-unionist independence from totalitarian rule became generalized opposition, in all area of social life. In economic matters, the union fought for higher wages and at the same time it advocated reforms which would give companies a broader margin of autonomy (it also supported employee self-management). New, representative peasant organisations developed under the trade union umbrella. Independent publishing houses came into being.

Massive grass-root support for Solidarity completely eroded what remained of the Party's ideological influence on society. As its influence waned the military, police and state security came into renewed prominence, and rule was simply by coercion.

The inevitable confrontation between Solidarity and the authorities came on 13 December 1981. Martial law was imposed and trade union activities were suspended but this merely signalled the start of a seven-year struggle of illegal trade-unionism and social protest against the power apparatus.

In the political sphere, various compromised organisations, including the old trade union structure, were wound up. New structures intended to be more independent (PRON – the Patriotic Movement for National Rebirth, OPZZ – the new official trade union organization, SDPRL – the journalists' association) but still connected with the authorities were established. New political institutions such as a Consultative Council to advise the government were set up and individual opposition activists invited to join in. An amnesty for political prisoners was declared and cultural policy was liberalized. These tactics however, failed to bring the desired results: the authorities were unable to gain the confidence of the population.

Throughout most of the 1980s the opposition urged resistance in the form of demonstrations and strikes while a fast deteriorating economic situation sapped social energy and channelled it into the defence of individual living standards. Eventually a wave of strikes in 1988 forced the authorities to sit at the negotiating table with diverse opposition groups, united under Solidarity colours.

The 'Round Table' talks of early 1989 produced a compromise. The Solidarity trade union was legalised again and a new set of rules was worked out providing for quasi-democratic elections to the Parliament in June 1989. None the less 65% of parliamentary seats were reserved for the former ruling coalition of the PZPR, the Peasants' Party and the Democratic Party. The remaining 35% were earmarked for so-called non-party candidates. A fully democratic election was to be held for the newly created house of the Parliament – the Senate, which had an advisory role.

Another element of the Round Table compromise was the restoration of a Presidency, with broad executive powers. An unwritten agreement provided for the appointment of General Wojciech Jaruzelski – the author of both martial law and the Round Table – to this post.

The real election campaign in June 1989 was concentrated on Senate and the 35% of non-party seats in Parliament. The Communist Party and the government side expected votes for candidates for non-party seats to be very dispersed. In the event, Solidarity put forward just one candidate for each seat

Elections were based on majority representation (more than 50% of votes cast in the first round). Solidarity won 99 out of the 100 seats in the Senate and all non-party seats in Parliament (161). A so-called 'national list' of leading figures linked with the authorities was a complete failure. Their names were consistently crossed out.

The election result transformed the political situation in the country.[3] Solidarity became unquestionably the leading political force in Poland. This proved decisive for subsequent developments. The election of the President by Parliament and Senate was the last act within the terms of the Round Table compromise. Many opposition parliamentarians abstained but even so General Jaruzelski was elected President by a majority of just one vote.

After June 1989 the pace of political developments accelerated. Following Wałęsa's initiative, the two parties formerly subordinated to the Polish United Workers' Party (the Peasants' Party and Democratic Party) left the old ruling coalition. Together with the parliamentary representation of Solidarity (in the so-called OKP – Citizens' Parliamentary Club) negotiations on the formation of a new government began. Mr Mazowiecki became prime minister and presided over a coalition of the OKP, the Peasants' Party, the Democratic Party and also of the PZPR, which retained the control of four ministries.

At the time it seemed that the PZPR still held the key elements of power: the President with the right to dissolve Parliament, the military and state security, supported by a state machinery staffed from top to bottom by party nominees, its so-called nomenklatura. However, the President soon found himself in a difficult position despite this and the PZPR was in any case quickly falling apart. Dramatic changes were also under way in the other European communist countries.

The opposition, which had been unified until then, also found itself in a new situation, and during 1989 two Solidarity factions emerged. Initially, the contentious issue was how to approach negotiations with the communist authorities but later, as the control of inflation became the top priority for the new Solidarity government, the dual position of Solidarity, as a trade union on the one hand and a social movement on the other, created a new dividing line. It is also worth bearing in mind here that Solidarity's 1989–90 membership amounted to only 20% of the 1980–1 figure.

Outside the parliamentary system various small political parties began to emerge. Several declared socialist sympathies others were centrist or liberal, still others nationalistic and Catholic. Thus far, their activities have been limited and they have had little social support. Up to early 1990 Polish society had not yet had time to identify with clear-cut political options. But the process of party formation was clearly well under way in the summer of 1990 as various rifts between Wałęsa and Mazowiecki as well as Wałęsa and Michnik came to prominence.

The situation in the peasent movement moved faster and is perhaps more clear cut. The United Peasants' Party (ZSL), formerly a member of the ruling coalition, changed its name and programme. It reached back for inspiration to the late 1940s, when under the name of the Polish Peasants' Party headed by the former prime minister of Poland's government in exile, Mikołajczyk, it opposed the Communists.

Two other peasant organisations created within the Solidarity movement also reached back to the same tradition. Despite the different origins of these organisations, there were clear signs they may jointly form a single party. They loudly (in mid-1990) articulated complaints and demands of private farmers form a natural starting point.

Summing up, at the threshold of the 1990s, a new political system had not yet replaced the old one, which was falling apart. But movement in that direction was clearly accelerating. This was to be expected: the decline of an old political structure is much more rapid than the birth of a new one. Polish society faced, in 1990, several possible political 'futures'.

3. Alternative political developments

Three groups of factors will bear on further political developments in Poland. First comes the international situation, especially the pace and directions of changes in the Soviet Union and the formerly socialist East European countries. Free parliamentary elections are widely promised. It might be anticipated that if they take place, the pace of changes will be much faster than in Poland. It may even be likely that this will contribute to *entirely* free elections being held in Poland sooner than expected, which will create a wholly new balance of political forces. Developments in the Soviet Union will no doubt have an important bearing on the situation in Poland and progress with perestroika will accelerate the collapse of the old political system. Should perestroika stop or slow down however, there is little doubt that it will also slow political reconstruction in the neighbouring countries.

Economic developments will be the second factor influencing further political changes. Costs incurred in curbing inflation and in the transformation of the economic system will bear on the social climate and on the extent of the opposition of certain key social groups (urban versus rural populations, employees against private capital, workers versus management). Higher 'anti-inflation' costs will mean more dramatic conflicts, as no social group will readily accept that pauperization is the price for economic transformations. If these contradictions become serious, they will no doubt help crystallize social support for different political parties and for competing elites connected with these parties.

The third element in the picture will be the pace of construction of the institutions of political democracy. Old political elites are retreating from their former ideological positions. The PZPR, which held its last congress in January 1990, split into two parties. Both call themselves social-democratic and both invoke the programmes of Western European counterparts. Further splits may follow. The Democratic Party aspires to a liberal platform, while the United Peasants' Party has already reached to the Catholic and agrarian values of the former Polish Peasants' Party.

Similar splits can also be observed within Solidarity. Social-democratic, liberal, peasant and nationalistic-Christian groups are consolidating themselves within the OKP and in the Senate. Outside Parliament there are some small political parties which basically represent similar orientations. This suggests the possible formation of a coalition, cutting across the present division based on the two extremes: the authorities and Solidarity. This process seems to be fastest in the peasant movement.

All in all, there is a vacuum yet to be filled, between the old ruling elite, new political elites and society. The new elite which rose from the Solidarity movement to form its first government, is now tied to society by thin strands of individual sympathies and support. The extent of this support is bound to decline because of the controversial decisions that the government must make.

Three possible alternative political futures for in Poland are worth considering:

3.1 Scenario one – economic success, Solidarity hangs together

Here the current situation, where democracy in political and social life is dominated by the Solidarity ethos, continues. This situation is only likely if the government's economic policy is successful. As inflation is curbed and output and incomes grow, social tensions would be considerably weakened. This could preserve the declining popularity of the Solidarity-dominated government and prevent a split within Solidarity ranks. Old political elites and the old ruling apparatus could be gradually and peacefully superseded. The next parliamentary election would consolidate a single, post-Solidarity power centre.

This political centre would be dominated by an ideology based on a combination of the social teachings of the Roman Catholic Church, a moderately liberal economic policy and social-democratic elements. Compromises would be worked out to take account of both national interests and those of various social groups.

Another aspect of this process would be that it would tend to check the rise of strong political parties. Various political groups would be unable to compete with the ruling coalition. They would probably take over some of the seats of the old parties in Parliament but would be unable to form a government on their own and implement different policies. This variant would also call for curbing the power both of the peasant movement and of the trade unions.

3.2 Scenario two – partial economic success, some Solidarity fragmentation

A partial economic success – the curbing of inflation achieved at the cost of a major decline in living standards – might contribute to a more rapid emergence of various social groups concerned mainly with defending living standards. In such a case, the parliamentary core of Solidarity would split into different political orientations. This would imply a rapid rise of political parties, and various coalitions formed across existing dividing lines. The position of the trade unions (Solidarność, OPZZ) would be enhanced, along with the role of organised interest groups (for example environmentalists). Proportional representation, which is likely to be adopted, would most likely result in bringing a wide spectrum of political orientations into Parliament, none of them able to rule alone. State policy would therefore be shaped by new coalitions, formed between these different groups.

3.3 Scenario three – economic failure, emerging authoritarianism

If the economic situation should go on deteriorating, then the conflict between various social groups may take on a destructive character. Authoritarian rule might emerge based on social conflicts deriving from new property relations and growing social inequality. Right-wing groups would provide the necessary ideology based on economic liberalism and nationalism. The support of a part of the Church hierarchy would be a necessary condition for this alternative to succeed. The 'need' to check the political but especially the economic aspirations of workers' organizations would be the main motive for restricting democracy.

A leftist and populist dictatorship seems much less likely. It would generate growing demands on the state especially as concerns distribution and attempts to implement it would lead to a social and economic anarchy that would open the door once again to right-wing authoritarianism.

Avoiding authoritarian rule calls for the creation of democratic institutions. In a situation where economic policy cannot ensure improved living standards it becomes crucial to tap all forms of social activity: individual enterprise, local democracy, social control over state property, development of parties and associations. If the vacuum is rapidly filled with active and well-organised interest groups in the forms of parties, associations, unions, then representative bodies will see their role enhanced and the establishment of authoritarian rule will be less likely.

There is a real danger however that the journey from communist rule towards political democracy might lead through another period of authoritarian rule.

Notes

1. The security services dominated in the years 1948–56. The next period saw the consolidation of the military and the economic administration, subordinated of course to the Party. During the 1970s the role of the party apparatus diminished as its legitimacy was called into even greater question. Instead, in the 1970s, structures which wielded real power – the state security, the economic administration (particularly some powerful industrial lobbies) – gained importance. It is somewhat ironic that just as its ideological rule was fading the principle of 'the leading role of the Party' was inscribed in the Constitution (1976).
2. They were described in Polish by the term 'stronnictwo' which many dictionaries translate as 'political party' for the lack of a better equivalent. In fact, a more accurate translation might be, 'group advocating something' or 'association'.
3. Although the outcome was unequivocal (Solidarity's victory) both sides were surprised with the relatively low participation in the first round. Instead of a widely expected 80% turnout the actual figure was 62%. Of these, 65% voted for Solidarity candidates. Thus Solidarity won over 40% of the popular vote while the authorities won less than 20%.

◆ CHAPTER 3 ◆

Poland: systemic reforms and economic policy in the 1980s

Dariusz K. Rosati

1. Introduction

The economic reforms of the 1980s may be interpreted by more sceptical obervers as yet another futile attempt to introduce greater rationality and efficiency to the Polish economy, plagued for many years by deep imbalances and chronic shortages. Those reforms were, after all, launched in an unfavourable political environment (martial law), and the experience from previous reform attempts was rather disappointing. At least two major reform programmes were undertaken before the 1980s, one in 1956–7 and another in 1971–2, but both proved to be short-lived and were quickly suspended without producing any significant change. The traditional economic system based on central planning dogma and collectivist ideology seemed to be infrangible, resisting quite successfully all reformist attempts.

And yet, the lessons of history may sometimes by deceptive. Developments in Poland in 1989–90 allow a much more optimistic outlook. In 1990 Poland embarked on a genuine systemic transformation aimed at establishing a Western-style free-market economy. It must be stressed however, that this remarkable change came about only after a prolonged period of intensive social and political struggle, and only after a fundamental shift in the balance of power.

The economic history of Poland after the Second World War is characterised by periods of accelerated growth (fuelled by extensive investment programmes) implemented at the cost of stagnating (or declining) consumption, followed by rapidly growing disequilibria and social discontent. This usually prompted more or less articulated calls for essential economic reform and often led to leadership changes. However, new leaders, once firmly in power, typically became increasingly reluctant to keep promises, trying instead to solve emerging economic problems with the use of traditional measures, like temporary reductions in the rate of investment, diverting resources from traditional sectors (agriculture) to industry, borrowing from abroad or simply printing more money. In a sense, therefore, the economic history of post war Poland is the history of 'relinquished reforms'.

There are several reasons for these repeated failures. The most important one was probably connected with the single-party/monocentric political system adopted in Poland in the late 1940s under pressure from the Soviet Union. This was based on centralized decision-making and overwhelming state control over the economy, whereas the fundamental idea of systemic reforms was always decentralization. These were obviously incompatible concepts, and their partial reconciliation was possible only for a very short time under conditions of emergency, when social pressure threatened the stability of the system.

Another reason for the lack of progress was that reform programmes suffered from numerous conceptual and operational weaknesses. With the benefit of hindsight one can see that reform ideas were frequently naive and simplistic. The international environment also impacted on the willingness and ability of successive governments to implement radical economic reforms. The 'Soviet factor' definitely played a crucial role in slowing down the reform process in Poland and elsewhere in the 1960s and 1970s.

In the 1980s political and international factors were decisive in determining the pace, scope and impact of the new wave of economic reforms in Poland. The 1980–1 reform was launched in a period of dramatic social change and quickly lost its momentum and got stuck in endless bureaucratic procedures and debates. Perhaps the main reason for that was a fundamental contradiction between the market-oriented, pro-efficiency reforms, and the general orientation of economic policy, dominated by short-term political considerations. Whereas the main objective of the former was to reconstruct the economic system to make it more flexible, more efficient and more outward-looking, the main goal of the latter was to maintain political control of the party-dominated bureaucratic apparatus over the economy.

2. The reform of 1981–2

At the turn of the 1980s the Polish economy ran into a deep economic and social crisis. A slow-down in growth and consumption which became more and more pronounced after 1975 provoked increased social discontent. Net Material Product fell by 2.3% in 1979 and by another 6% in 1980, foreign debt rose from $8.4 bn in 1975 to $25 bn in 1980 and annual price inflation steadily increased from 2% or 3% in 1971–5 to 7% or 9% in 1978–80. At the same time the market situation deteriorated, with ever greater food and consumer good shortages.

The underlying symptoms were typical for a centrally-planned economy entering its cyclical downswing. Polish economists were almost unanimous in explaining the crisis with two principal causes: the rigid, centralized and bueaucratic economic system and the 'voluntarist', irresponsible economic policy of the Gierek Jaroszewicz government. There were, however, significant differences in emphasis: while the first cause was strongly emphasised by more reform-oriented economists and by the political opposition, the second cause was favoured by conservatives. This distinction was crucial for the further development of the process of reforms: it marked a recognition of the difference between systemic changes and policy adjustments, and more important, it opened a long period of controversy among economists and politicians over the required pattern and scope of reforms. As may be seen from the Polish experience in the 1980s, these controversies and disputes led invariably to compromises which seriously weakened the emerging market mechanism.

Faced by falling output and exports, drastic market shortages, and mounting social pressure, the Polish government prepared a new programme of radical economic reforms during 1980–1 and aimed for its implementation from the beginning of 1982. After almost one year of intensive debate, the final blueprint of the reform was approved by Parliament on 25 September 1981. The general idea of the reform was to reduce considerably the extent of direct controls over the economy, and to replace them with a variety of indirect economic measures working through the market mechanism.

The most important element of the programme was undoubtedly the elimination of central planning, accompanied by greater autonomy for state enterprises (see 'Law on Socio-Economic Planning' of 26 February 1982). Enterprises were freed from compulsory targets imposed from above and allowed to set their own production and sales programmes. They were also given (limited) powers to decide on the distribution of profits and incomes. Firms were to cover costs with sales revenues and inputs were to be available through regular commercial transactions, thus breaking with the traditional rationing system.

Planning was not however to be scrapped altogether. On the contrary, the system of multi-period plans was to be maintained, and the programme actually explicitly called for 'strengthening national planning's strategic functions'. The government was obliged to prepare a so-called 'Central Annual Plan' (CPR) every year as well as a 'National Socio-Economic Plan (NPSG) every five years. Both were to be approved by Parliament. While planned targets were not formally compulsory for enterprises except for some specific areas (military and state security activities, fulfilment of trade agreements with the CMEA countries), a number of additional legal regulations severely limited the real independence of enterprises. There was still great scope for administrative distribution of many materials, inputs and machinery in short supply. Firms were also obliged to provide government agencies with detailed information about production and investment programmes. Moreover, managers of state companies continued to be dependent informally on higher level authorities.

In 1982 a new law promised that prices were to be set by the market mechanism, through the interaction of demand and supply. Administrative price controls were indeed lifted for a majority of products but important restrictions remained, covering, among others, coal, fuel, energy, steel products, cement, fertilizers, basic consumer goods and services as well as procurement prices for agricultural products paid to private farmers. For these goods so-called 'administrative prices' (ceny urzędowe) were applied. Some other prices, although not directly fixed by the government, were subject to indirect controls and still could not be set freely by producers (so-called 'regulated prices' – ceny regulowane).

An important provision in the new law stipulated that prices for primary goods would be fixed at the level corresponding to international prices. As it turned out, this principle was not implemented, and until 1990 prices for primary commodities were held below international levels.

More significant changes were introduced into the foreign trade system. The so-called 'state monopoly of foreign trade' was formally dismantled, and all enterprises, public or private, could apply for a licence to export or import. A licence was available provided specific conditions were fulfilled, concerning the minimum share of exports in total output (20%) or, alternatively, the minimum required level of annual export sales (initially the limit was set at zł 1 bn, equivalent to $12.5 mn). Another condition required a potential exporter to prove that it possessed 'sufficient' professional and technical expertise to trade internationally. This point, like many others, opened the way for considerable discretion in the licence-granting process.

A new exchange rate regime was established, the underlying principle of which was to peg the złoty at the ('sub-marginal') level ensuring the profitability of 75% to 85% of exports. Convertibility was the ultimate goal. Perhaps the most significant innovation in the new system was that exporters could retain a proportion of their hard currency export earnings and spend the sums as needed on imports. Export retention quotas[1] ranged from 2% to 50% of export earnings and became an important incentive for export expansion. However no specific provisions for the creation of a foreign exchange market were made within the 1980–1 scheme and most foreign exchange was still rationed.

3. Reform and economic policy – measures in collision

The 1982 economic reform was implemented in an extremely difficult environment. Increasing social tensions, widespread strikes and political confrontation between the communist-led government and Solidarity-led opposition left the economy in 1981 on the threshold of total collapse. Martial law was imposed on 13 December 1981 replacing growing chaos with the military rule which suspended civil rights and cut off the country from external markets. The year 1982 marked the trough of the crisis: produced NMP was 17% lower than in 1980 and 24% below the peak of 1978, but distributed NMP (NMP corrected by the trade balance) fell by 20% and 27.5% respectively. Imports fell by 22.5% as compared with 1978, but imports from Western countries shrunk by more than 50%!

As the data in Table 3.1 show, after the deep slump of 1980–1, the Polish economy registered a relatively strong recovery in 1983–4. NMP rose by 12%, as did industrial output, and the long-standing trade deficit was transformed to a surplus of $1.2 bn to $1.4 bn annually. The official view held, optimistically (and mistakenly), that these data were a symptom of a long-term, sustainable recovery brought about thanks to the economic reform. Armed with this argument, the government vigorously defended itself against proponents of

Table 3.1 The economy 1981–8
(Preceding year = 100)

	1981	1982	1983	1984	1985	1986	1987	1988
NMP produced	88.0	94.5	106.0	105.6	103.4	104.9	101.9	104.9
NMP distributed	89.5	89.5	105.6	105.0	103.8	105.0	101.8	104.7
NMP/per capita (produced)	87.2	93.6	105.0	104.6	102.6	104.2	101.4	104.3
NMP/per capita (distributed)	88.7	88.7	104.6	104.1	103.0	104.2	101.3	104.2
Industrial output	86.8	98.5	106.6	105.6	104.1	104.4	103.4	105.3
Gross Product deflator	118.9	209.5	114.2	113.8	117.3	118.0	127.0	165.6
Consumer price index	121.2	204.5	121.4	114.8	115.0	117.5	125.3	161.3
Investment	77.7	87.9	109.4	111.4	106.0	105.1	104.2	105.4
Share of the private sector in NMP*	30.4	20.0	19.6	18.8	18.2	18.2	17.2	18.8

* current prices
Source: Central Statistical Office (GUS)

more fundamental and more radical systemic changes. The reality, however, was different.

The recovery turned out to be temporary and short-lived. In 1985 growth rates declined considerably both in the domestic and export sectors, and internal disequilibrium widened. One of the reasons was probably the attempt to accelerate growth through greater investment in 1984. This failed, and the most obvious explanation is the lack of any fundamental breakthrough in the reform process.

The apparent recovery of 1983–4 was mainly the result of a restoration of elementary discipline in the economy after a period of strikes and political struggle in 1980–1. This allowed higher capacity utilization. A substantial increase of coal production – Poland's chief export – was achieved thanks to significant wage increases in mining. Reduced domestic demand also gave some scope for export growth though this was mainly evident in Comecon trade. Finally, part of the 'credit' for recovery should go to the fact that the economy started from an extremely low output and exports base.

Output and foreign trade difficulties intensified in 1986–7. To revitalize obsolete industrial sectors and to reduce their high energy and material intensity, new investment and new technologies were needed. This was not feasible however as both domestic and foreign sources of capital were still very limited. Meanwhile social restiveness grew over dissatisfaction with low living standards and lack of progress in political reforms. The Polish economy, caught between twin evils of domestic and external disequilibrium, was relentlessly sliding down into another deep crisis.

Official propaganda tried to blame the unfavourable external environment (sanctions) and the domestic political opposition for the slow pace of economic reform. A more plausible explanation however lies with the strong resistance of the administrative and party apparatus to any real decentralization. The 1980s governments of Jaruzelski and Messner, though recognizing to some extent that insufficient progress was due to political constraints, were unable to overcome this barrier. Economic policy in 1982–8 was dominated not by economic objectives, like efficiency, rationality and growth, but by political considerations. The fundamental objective of the government was simply to stay in power at any price – and the price was a gradual collapse of the national economy.

Economic policy often requires difficult and politically hazardous choices and trade-offs to be made over income distribution. In Poland, urgent decisions were in most cases delayed and unpopular measures simply avoided. Faced, for example, with the choice of imposing price controls or allowing the market mechanism to set prices at equilibrium levels, the government opted invariably for the first solution, regarding it as politically safe in the short term. Struggling over restructuring of Polish industry, the government would implement hugely bureaucratic reorganization schemes, rather than permit the market mechanism to work and allow inefficient state-owned companies to go bankrupt. Admitting verbally the need for substantial reallocation of manpower, the government nevertheless would not permit any open unemployment. Short-term political considerations and ideological dogma paralysed any attempt to introduce genuine market mechanisms.

Economic policy requires sensitive judgement to be exercised in establishing a balance between efficiency in production and social justice in income distribution. In Poland, egalitarian tendencies usually had the upper hand and decisions on income distribution were subordinated to political goals. Fiscal policy, for example, led to excessive income redistribution from efficient companies to inefficient ones. Wages and salaries tended to be highest in large industrial enterprises and little connected to profitability or productivity.

Economic policy also needs careful judgement as to choice of instruments. In Poland, until 1989, policy was always inclined towards excessive use of direct administrative measures, displaying a consistent disregard for indirect, parametric measures. The domination of administrative allocation systems for many essential inputs, capital goods and foreign exchange, and a reluctance to rely more on market forces, followed logically from the political preferences of the government, but the economic outcome proved disastrous. Short-sighted, politically motivated and inconsistent policies blocked and neutralized those few market mechanisms introduced in 1982. Prices and wages were not regulated by the market. Exchange rates and interest rates were strictly controlled and kept at artificially low levels. Numerous administrative restrictions did not allow any significant structural change in the economy. Under these conditions, the Polish economy was trapped in a systemic 'vacuum', where neither central plan nor market operated.

4. The failure of the 'second stage' of the reform and the crisis of 1988–9

The notion of a 'second stage' of the reform was launched in late 1986 as a reaction to growing imbalances and slowdown in the Polish economy. The authorities realized that a major breakthrough was needed to reverse the downward trend. The emphasis was initially put on accelerating already scheduled reforms and reworking the 1982 blueprint.

The failure to break away from old management styles was demonstrated clearly during the preparation of the five-year plan for 1986–90, where both targets and instruments were formulated in a traditional manner. The plan actually assumed the strengthening of central government controls over the economy, further expansion of heavy industries, especially coal mining and energy production, and a practical freeze on economic relations with the West. The plan did not propose any increased reliance on market mechanisms to improve resource allocation and economic efficiency.

This blueprint stirred a heated discussion among economists and policy makers alike, but despite extensive criticisms it was eventually approved by Parliament in 1986. This plan showed just how strongly the central bureaucracy would defend its interests and also how desperately narrow-minded and naive official reform concepts were.

So, despite another opportunity to move forward in the mid 1980s, the major drawbacks of the original reform concept from 1982 were not eliminated. Reform proposals still avoided major market economy institutions such as a capital or foreign exchange market. Second, economic policy was still dominated by a traditional approach, favouring administrative measures and excessive 'fiscalism', and overlooked monetary and credit policy, as well as an exchange rate policy.

As a result, the 'second stage' of the economic reform had few genuine innovations. But some that did creep in included a long-awaited joint-venture law (approved by Parliament in 1986), limited foreign exchange auctions (worth only $9.1 mn in 1987) and, with the elimination of some ministries, a streamlining of central government. The ministerial reorganization was however largely neutralized by the immediate establishment of monopolistic structures in heavy industries (so-called 'Wspólnota'), which effectively assumed powers from old ministries.

Economic policy was also extremely conservative. Attempts to stabilize the economy were based mainly on traditional measures: price and wage controls, taxation and direct allocation of resources (especially of capital and foreign exchange). To make matters worse other policies (especially state spending) were highly inflationary.

Although formal price controls were in force only for some 20% of products (mostly primary commodities and basic consumer goods), up to 70% of products were subject to some kind of indirect price control (through the so-called 'contract' – ceny umowne – price system), for example through the compulsory notification of intended price increases, or the discretionary ruling by government agencies as to when price increases were 'excessive'. The efficiency of these indirect controls was low and as a result a 'dual' price system emerged, with some 'contract' prices rising very fast and some 'administered' prices remaining fixed for prolonged periods. This resulted in increased distortions and growing shortages, coupled with higher inflation.

Income policy was traditionally tax-based and was again very inefficient for a number of reasons. First, the government was not able to resist wage pressures from big enterprises and from 'branch' lobbies. Second, Kornai's famous 'soft' budget constraint allowed many enterprises to finance excessive manpower costs with bank credit, inter-enterprise credits, or with direct grants from the budget. Third, there was no political will within the government to cut real wages. As a result wages and salaries were growing faster than prices, fuelling inflation.

Fiscal policies were dominated by excessive enterprise taxation on one hand, and by lack of discipline in state spending on the other hand. Enterprises not only were supposed to pay profits tax of 45% to 60% but also a large part of the depreciation fund was to be surrendered to the state budget. At the same time a substantial redistribution of income through the tax system was taking place in the form of transfer of funds from efficient units (mostly medium and small size manufacturers) to inefficient ones (big heavy industry enterprises) in the form of tax reliefs and direct subsidies. Subsidies constituted the most important single item in the government budget and their share grew from some 25% in 1983–4 to 36% in 1988.

Monetary and credit policy was however relaxed and passive. The money supply accomodated immediate needs, dictated frequently by the desire to 'buy' social support. This policy intensified especially in 1988 and 1989, when political tensions grew and Mr Rakowski's government assumed office. State spending was not directly dependent on actual revenues, and could always be financed through non-interest-bearing credit from the National Bank of Poland. This system of money creation led to very low financial and monetary discipline, and was an important source of inflation.

Similarly, exchange rate policy was passive. The official dollar rate was held much below the equilibrium rate, securing the profitability of not more than 65% of convertible currency exports. That was accompanied by an extensive price equalization system, whereby losses and profits on foreign trade transactions were settled by the central budget via differential taxes-cum-subsidies. In the presence of a notoriously overvalued exchange rate, numerous restrictions on the convertibility of the złoty had to be maintained in order to protect the fragile balance of payments. Although złoty convertibility was a policy objective after 1981, it remained an elusive goal in the 1980s. Over 1984–8 the share of centrally allocated foreign exchange fell from 70% to 61%.

An overview of economic policy in the mid 1980s shows that it was not only ineffective in restoring domestic and external balance, but it was also inconsistent with the spirit of the systemic reforms. While the latter aimed at establishing an efficient market economy (albeit still with a modified planning system with a relatively high degree of government intervention) the former was subordinated to the political objective of maintaining maximum control over the economy. As a result, pro-market reforms, even if introduced formally by parliamentary legislation, remained in practice 'on paper'.

The inconsistency between reform and policy had of course its roots in the political set up. The government was not trusted by the population and more radical measures to stop inflation and eliminate shortages would probably have provoked large-scale social protests. What appeared still feasible and not too costly in terms of anti-inflationary policy in 1982–4, became definitely politically unfeasible and economically too demanding in 1986–9. The government was in a cul-de-sac. Although formally committed to market reforms, it was not prepared to accept the concomitant reduction in its powers. Lack of popular support and pressure from the political opposition further diminished the readiness and willingness of the government to speed up any genuine reform process. This reform 'paralysis' was the main reason for the lack of progress in overcoming the Polish crisis.

5. The new economic programme 1990: stabilization and institutional transformation

The changes which have been taking place in Poland since the 'Round Table' in April 1989 are unprecedented. This is not a simple policy adjustment; it is a fundamental systemic transformation of historical significance. The principal objective of this transformation is to switch from a totalitarian system based on the rule of one party to a democratic, multi-party system, and from a centrally-planned economy to a competitive market economy, based on private ownership of capital and guided by efficiency criteria and the profit motive.

The new economic programme, launched by the Mazowiecki government on 1 January 1990, is a bold attempt to stabilize the Polish economy and to establish the institutional basis for a competitive market mechanism. The programme has two elements: a stabilization package, aimed at bringing down inflation and restoring market equilibrium, and an institutional (systemic) transformation, aimed at creating in Poland a modern market economy of the type prevailing in the West. While the first part is short term the second part constitutes a comprehensive restructuring of the institutional framework of the Polish economy and is of necessity long term.

While planning the implementation of the programme, the government had to decide on two important policy issues. Firstly, confronted with the choice between a gradual, step-by-step implementation and 'shock' treatment, the government decided on the second approach, on the grounds that with the Polish economy on the threshold of total collapse there was simply no time to lose. Secondly, the government decided to implement the two parts simultaneously.

The stabilization package was regarded by both domestic and international

experts as radical and ambitious. It included five main components:
- the freeing, in January 1990, of almost all remaining administrative price controls, coupled with the increase of official coal and energy prices by 400% to 600% and other fuel prices by roughly 100%;
- the so-called 'internal convertibility' of the złoty, that is, the unification of the market for foreign exchange for most current transactions, accompanied by a sharp official devaluation of the złoty by 32% from zł 6,500/$ to zł 9,500/$, with the aim (successfully achieved) of maintaining the fixed exchange rate for at least six months;
- the limitation of wage fund growth in enterprises to a small fraction of the price inflation (0.3 in January, 0.2 in February–April) through a very restrictive tax-based income indexation policy (also successfully implemented);
- the elimination of the budget deficit and attainment of approximate fiscal balance by the general government in 1990, through major cuts in food and commodity subsidies, reductions of public investment programmes and defence and internal security expenditures, coupled with substantial increase of taxes, custom duties and other fiscal charges paid by enterprises.
- a major tightening of credit and monetary policy, through a strict limitation of the rate of domestic credit expansion to government and non-government sectors, together with a sharp increase of interest rates making them positive in real terms.

On the systemic side some changes were introduced from the beginning of 1990 with others to follow in 1991. The main elements of the systemic package include:
- the rapid privatization of state-owned or co-operative enterprises, through competitive asset sales;
- breaking up existing monopolies and creating favourable conditions for unrestricted competition among enterprises, from both private and public sectors;
- liberalization of foreign trade and payments, removing most administrative restrictions on the licensing of foreign trade and establishing a foreign exchange market;
- liberalization of the land market;
- modernization of the financial sector through creation of a two-tier banking system, with a network of strong and competitive commercial banks, applying modern technologies and techniques of banking operations;
- establishment of a fully-fledged capital market, with a stock exchange;
- modification of the Labour Code to establish conditions for a labour market;
- upgrading the managerial and administration skills of the Polish business community, through extensive training programmes organized jointly with foreign institutions;
- a comprehensive reform of the tax system, aimed at the introduction of a broad-based individual income tax and replacement of differential turnover taxes with a value-added tax;

– a new joint-venture law, offering significant incentives for foreign investors.

The general orientation of the programme is neo-liberal and neo-monetarist in character. In fact, it follows rather closely the standard IMF approach to macroeconomic stabilization policy, and, not surprisingly, has been highly praised by IMF and World Bank officials.

At the time of writing, three months into the programme, its comprehensive evaluation is impossible, but some preliminary observations can be made. It seems that the programme has displayed both merits and faults. While the general philosophy and the approach applied is correct, the sequencing and the internal structure of the package could have been better designed.

The most spectacular success is perhaps the complete elimination of hyper inflation. While consumer prices jumped by 78.6% in January, they slowed down remarkably in February (23.8%), and again in March (4.7%). Another undoubted success was the stabilization of the złoty without recourse to excessively administrative restrictions on imports. After three months the foreign exchange market seemed to be in balance, without any central bank intervention, and without drawing either IMF credits or on the $1 bn stabilization fund set up by leading Western nations to defend the złoty. On the domestic market goods are readily available (if expensive) and shortages have disappeared. Finally, the central budget remained in equilibrium.

However, there are also some negative effects. The most serious one is the drastic decline of output (25% to 30% in January–March 1990 as compared with the corresponding period of 1989). Such a deep recession was not expected: it showed that the anti-inflationary and stabilization measures initially applied were probably too restrictive. Unemployment reached 250,000 at the end of March (and approached half a million in mid summer 1990) and more companies found themselves in a critical financial position, staring financial ruin in the face. True, both unemployment and bankruptcies are inevitable side effects of the extensive restructuring of the economy, but if they reach unacceptable levels, the government may find it difficult to contain social discontent. The significant drop in real wages (31.6% over the first quarter of 1990) was testing to the limit Solidarity government's popular support. Finally, some key sectors were hit especially, and again unexpectedly, hard by the programme. These included agriculture, light industry, housing and foreign trade (particularly imports).

It seemed, after the first quarter of 1990, that to avoid unnecessary economic and social cost, and in order to allow for more response on the supply side, that some sort of adjustment in the programme was becoming desirable. The government may decide to soften its wages policy and cut taxes to stimulate production and supply, while still maintaining a fairly tight monetary and credit policy. The acceleration of legislative work on the institutional framework to support the market mechanism, lagging behind the stabilization measures, is also of crucial importance.[2]

6. Conclusion

Irrespective of what course will be taken by the government in the near future, there is growing evidence that its programme may be successful. While the sequence and intensity of particular measures may still be questioned and debated, there are two important pillars which provide a solid basis for guarded optimism. One is the support promised by Western countries in the form of financial and economic aid. This includes financial assistance from the IMF (a stand-by loan arrangement of $750 mn), the stabilization fund to support the Polish currency, and the aid programme financed by the EEC. The second crucial pillar of the economic programme was the popular support which Mazowiecki's government has enjoyed in Poland since it assumed office in September 1989. Despite the unquestionable harshness of the economic programme, public opinion polls showed, in April 1990, that more than 70% of people sampled supported the government. However, the readiness of the Polish nation to accept these sacrifices, and the determination of the government to continue with radical reforms cannot be stretched beyond limits. The West may therefore need to step up its assistance for Poland in order to alleviate this difficult transition period. The final outcome of the programme is still in the balance but never before has Poland had such an opportunity to stabilize its strained economy and establish a strong base for sustainable growth in the future.

Notes

1. These were known as ROD accounts from the Polish 'rachunki odpisów dewizowych' – literally foreign exchange deduction account.
2. In early June 1990 the government reviewed economic policy and performance in the first half of the year and did make adjustments designed to take the sting out of the recession and to stimulate a stronger supply-side response – Eds.

♦ CHAPTER 4 ♦

Environment

Michal Rusiński

1. Introduction

During the last few decades Poland's socio-economic development has relied heavily on an extensive exploitation of the country's resources of water, minerals, forests and soils. This has produced far-reaching environmental degradation and disruption of the ecological balance. Health standards have been critically jeopardized. Today, environmental awareness is increasing dramatically and it is widely accepted that the underlying cause of the current predicament is the one-dimensional development strategy aimed, over the postwar years, at accelerated industrialization. Radical policy shifts are badly needed but they must take place in extremely unfavourable conditions.

In this chapter we discuss the current environmental crisis and outline basic policy options. The formulation of any sensible predictions in this respect is highly risky. The extent of environmental damage, as well as the resources which might be allocated to environmental protection, depends heavily on future growth and structural change in the economy.

The system of collecting, processing and making public information on the state of the environment in Poland suffers from numerous deficiencies and inconsistencies. It is widely known that data published by the Central Statistical Office are incomplete.[1] This is not because of the statistical methods applied or of computing deficiencies but rather due to underdeveloped environmental monitoring. Only a negligible part (5%) of the relevant data come from direct environmental monitoring whereas in the Netherlands or Nordic countries direct monitoring typically accounts for one half of available environmental data. In Poland most data are derived from enterprises, that is from the polluters themselves. Moreover, only a few firms have been obliged to report on a regular basis, and small plants have not been covered at all. The emissions of farms, recreation centres, hospitals and workshops have not been monitored. Only the 1,362 'particularly harmful' plants – the major air polluters – have been monitored regularly, and this covers only one tenth of the total number of known sources of toxic emissions.

Notwithstanding the poor methodological and technical basis of environmental statistics, the existing data paint a bleak picture in air and water pollution and abatement, soil degradation and contamination, industrial and municipal waste discharge, deforestation, landscape protection, land use and protection of flora and fauna.

2. Environmental dislocation

Poland is undoubtedly one of the most heavily polluted countries in Europe, particularly as far as emissions of gaseous pollutants and particles, industrial waste and the treatment level of discharged effluent are concerned. Nor, it should be noted, do the aggregate and average figures reflect properly the gravity of the situation. The intensity of pressure on the environment is also strongly regionally differentiated. Previous Polish governments identified twenty-seven 'ecologically threatened areas' covering as much as 11% of the country's territory with 35% of the population. Living conditions there are extremely hard, and cannot be expected to improve even in the medium term. There the ecological balance has been totally disrupted and the health hazards are considerable.

The 'threatened areas' category was introduced for planning purposes in 1983. They have an average population density of 380 persons per square km, three times the country average. About 61% of the country's industrial and municipal effluent and 58% of non-treated waste water, 75% of dust emission and 80% of gaseous pollutants falls on these areas. Some 93% of total waste is deposited there, that is about 40 tons per square km. The situation in Silesia is particularly dramatic. Out of a population of 4 million, some 3 million live in an 'ecologically threatened area' and 1 million are exposed to pollution levels many times exceeding those officially allowed (for example, for dust particles in the air actual concentration is 40 times the 'allowable' norm, for nitrogen oxides it is 7 times, for carbon monoxide it is 50 times, for lead and benzo-a-piren it is 60 times). On an area equal to 2% of Poland's territory, with a population density 5 times higher than the average, some 4,000 big and medium-sized enterprises are located, and among them can be found one quarter of the 900 most serious Polish polluters.[2]

In 1988, outside the ecological hazard areas some deceleration of pollution growth was registered, and in some cases its growth was halted. However, even in those cases stabilization was achieved at a very high pollution level. This was the case for dust and sulphur dioxide in the air and for waste water discharges. The area of degraded and devastated land has fallen slightly. However, in many other spheres no tangible progress has been achieved. The most troublesome were:

– accelerated forest decline, due to insufficient control of noxious air pollutants from indigenous sources, particularly of sulphur dioxide, nitrogen oxides, hydrocarbons, other dust matter and fluorine compounds. The situation

was aggravated by the massive inflow of transborder pollution, especially from the GDR and Czechoslovakia,
- lack of progress in slowing the growth of municipal and industrial wastes deposited in the environment,
- degradation of water resources in rural areas, and the concomitant deterioration of sanitary conditions in the countryside,
- progressive soil degradation, stemming from undue and improper application of fertilizers and pesticides, resulting in an increased chemical contamination of foodstuffs, and especially vegetables.

The current state of the Polish environment is described below.

2.1. *Atmospheric pollution and protection*

Some 60% to 70% of total air pollution originates in power stations, chemical plants, and from the metallurgy and building materials industry. Only 10% to 15% of emissions are generated by transport, especially road transport.

In 1988 Polish industry and power generation discharged some 5.2 mn tons of gaseous pollutant into the air, including 2.8 mn tons of sulphur dioxide (United Nations Economic Commission for Europe (UNECE) estimates are much higher), 1.4 mn tons of carbon monoxide, 0.8 mn tons of nitrogen oxides and more than 0.2 mn tons of other particularly hazardous and toxic substances.

Dust emission amounts to 1.6 mn tons, including some 96,000 tons of metallurgical dust, containing, among others, toxic compounds of heavy metals. Poland has one of the worst records among European countries with regard to heavy metals pollution. In 1982, with 15% of total European cadmium emission Poland ranked second in Europe, with 6% of mercury emission it held fourth place and with 4% of total lead emission it was seventh in Europe. Recently a slow, but systematic decrease (at 3% per annum over 1980-7) of dust emission from big industrial plants has occurred. Nevertheless norms for the annual concentration of suspended dust were violated in as many as 97% of monitoring points, and in 77% of all points were more than five times higher than permitted.[3] The dominant role of sulphur dioxide in the global emission of gaseous pollutants, amounting to 54%, results from the specific structure of power generation in Poland which is 80% based on hard coal and lignite combustion. Sulphur dioxide emission is the second highest in Europe. Some 10% of all European sulphur dioxide emission and 8% of nitrogen oxides emission is generated on Polish territory. While in Europe in the first half of the 1980s a substantial reduction of about 15% was achieved, environmental control in Poland managed to contribute only to a stabilization of emission at a high level.[4] Only some 15% of gaseous pollutants from industrial sources and power generation was brought under control (in power generation only 3%, in metallurgy 33% and in the chemical industry 46%). This share is very low as compared for example with 95% for dust emission brought under control.

Some 40% of sulphur dioxide and as much as 75% of nitrogen oxides deposited on Polish territory are 'imported' predominantly from the south and west. Also the emission of heavy metals like cadmium, chromite, mercury and lead has remained high as compared with other European countries. One-third of lead emission was generated by automobiles.

The emission of atmospheric pollutants, particularly sulphur dioxide, has been growing for many years. It has to be emphasized that even the economic crisis at the turn of 1970s and 1980s did not dent this trend. In 1980–2 when industrial production fell by nearly 14% the emission of atmospheric pollutants declined by 11% and gaseous pollutants by only 7%. This adverse tendency causes great concern, particularly when compared with divergent trends of economic growth and emissions achieved in most Western industrialized countries.[5]

2.2. *Water resources and management*

Total water resources in Poland amount to 63 cubic kilometres and disposable resources to 22 cubic kilometres. Only roughly 6% of annual river run-off can be stored in reservoirs. In 1988 a total of 14.3 cubic kilometres of water was utilised, 68% for industrial users, 21% for municipal and 11% for agricultural consumers. Surface waters met 84% of total water demand. Per capita water utilisation and consumption amounted to 407 cubic metres. From among 4,886 plants operating water-intensive production lines only 1,769 were equipped with water recirculation systems (closed circuits). The volume of industrial and municipal waste-water discharged to surface waters amounted to 12.1 cubic kilometres, including 4.5 cubic kilometres of waste-water requiring treatment. This figure omits cooling waters in power generation, which often are polluted quite badly by oils or lubricants and may need treatment.

About 37% of water discharges occurred without any treatment. From the total volume of waste-water treated, some 55% were treated exclusively with the use of mechanical techniques, and as little as 37% with the application of biological processes. Some 48% of industrial plants were devoid of any purification facilities, 110 towns went without any urban sewage system, and 374 towns without any sewage treatment facilities. In recent years the volume of industrially discharged waste-water requiring treatment has fallen slightly, and some two hundred purification plants have gone into operation annually. Most rural sewage however is still discharged practically untreated to surface waters and into the ground. The more widespread application of detergents, pesticides and chemical fertilizers puts heavy pressure on water quality. This inhibits its improvement and the quality of Poland's principal rivers – the Vistula and Oder – has been declining steadily for more than twenty years.

First-class quality water runs only on 4.2% of total river length where water quality has been monitored. Water quality is below *any* standard on as much as 40% of river length and is unsuitable for any economic use. This poor quality of surface waters has been the decisive factor in the rapid degradation of the coastal marine environment of the Baltic Sea. Poland has certainly played its part in the pollution of Baltic waters. The discharged effluent load in terms of biological oxygen demand $(BOD_5)^6$ is around 22% of the total pollution load discharged by all seven Baltic states. Pollution of ground water has also been increasing and this is even more disturbing as this water has been used primarily for drinking purposes. As far as effluent treatment is concerned, the situation in Poland is particularly unfavourable as compared with other countries. The direct comparative assessment of water quality in Poland and in other European countries is hardly possible, due to the lack of adequate data and different classification systems. However if waters with a BOD_5 index not higher than 4 mg O_2/l are classified as clear, than approximately 50% of European river waters meet this standard, but only 5% in Poland.

2.3. Land use and waste disposal

The total surface of devastated and degraded land requiring reclamation and development amounted to 100,000 hectares at the end of 1988, and only 3,700 hectares, that is less than 4%, has been recultivated. Owing to changes in land use, the total area of biologically active land fell by some 140,000 hectares in the period 1980–7. Soils are contaminated with many noxious chemical substances (for example, sulphur, zinc, cadmium, lead), endangering seriously the health of humans and animals alike.

In 1988 a total of 186 mn tons of industrial waste was generated, from which only 57% was utilized and a mere 0.2% neutralized. About 43% of waste volume were deposited at permanent storage sites. The accumulated volume of waste amounted to 1.5 bn tons and exceeded by 2.5 times that of 1975. Industrial waste originating in mining dominated. The total discharge of municipal waste to 'official' storage sites (predominantly shallow landfills) increased in the same period by three times. However, the 'wild' storage of domestic agricultural and even industrial waste is very frequent, although illegal and prosecuted. International comparative data confirm the leading place of Poland in industrial waste generation particularly from heavy industry and power generation.

2.4. Forests, flora, fauna, nature and landscape protection

Forests cover 27.7% of Poland's territory. The coniferous monocultures, particularly vulnerable to damage caused by pollution, dominate. There has been a particularly dramatic and rapid decay of forests in the southern and south-western parts of the country, along the German and Czechoslovak borders. This process has produced substantial political and social tensions; some steps at intergovernmental level have been taken and a certain degree of understanding on the part of Poland's neighbours was reached. Still, the problem is far from solved. In Poland in 1987 only 24.4% of coniferous and 46.6% of leafy standing timber remained undamaged. Some 64% of forest area is damaged by industrial pollutants. Forest decay and general flora and fauna degradation is characteristic for the whole of Europe. Apart from Poland (the Sudety mountains, Silesian industrial area, Pulawy and the surrounding countryside), large areas of decaying coniferous forests exist in the GDR, Czechoslovakia, the Federal Republic of Germany and Austria. Forests surrounding industrial plants in all countries of Central Europe (Poland, the GDR, Czechoslovakia, the Federal Republic of Germany, Austria, Switzerland) as well as in France, Spain, Yugoslavia, Romania and Sweden are seriously damaged.

In 1988 the total area of legally protected land (national parks, landscape parks and nature reserves) amounted to 4.5 mn hectares equivalent to 14.3% of Polish territory. The fourteen existing national parks cover only 0.4% of the area of Poland. All of them (and especially those located in the mountains) have been exposed to heavy airborne pollution, and one half to the stress of industrial and municipal effluent and run-off of dissolved chemicals from crop lands.

3. Environmental protection – current state and prospects

This necessarily brief description shows clearly the vast scale of the environmental problem in Poland, with which environmental policy has been confronted and has to cope. It demands prompt mobilization of large resources and their efficient use. However, trends in financing environmental control in Poland are not especially comforting. According to the Central Statistical Office, investment expenditures for environmental protection were 17% lower in 1988 than stipulated by the Central Annual Plan, and those connected with air pollution control were even 40% lower. In 1987 the investment shortfall was 9% of the planned volume. Also, the share of environmental investment in national income (0.8%) remained almost unchanged. In many countries this share amounts to as much as 3% to 6%.

In 1988 investment in environmental protection totalled zł 61.4 bn and was 6% greater than in 1987. Its share in total investment in the non-private economy amounted to 3.5% and was sourced as follows: central budget – 14.5%, local budgets – 22.1%, enterprises' own funds – 52.4%, subsidies from special ecological funds about 11%. As regards the structure of funds allocated, water management dominated (63%), then land protection (with waste management) 20%, and air pollution control had about 17%. This distribution was far from compatible with the structure of needs, which were most urgent in air protection.

Money collected from enterprises in the form of charges and penalties has been set aside in special ecological funds, recently merged to build the National Fund of Environmental Protection and Water Management, but the ecological funds set up has been heavily criticized. The main problem was its limitation to simple subsidization of environmental investments. The new unified Fund will acquire a legal basis, its own board and will be allowed to engage in credit activity, in participation in joint stock companies, in buying shares and bonds, and will also set up specialised 'innovating' enterprises to introduce new technologies. It will operate as a kind of eco-bank. But adequate and well-used finance is only one of many components in an effective system of environmental protection. Such a system, after all, has been under construction in Poland for many years, and much lip service has been paid to environmental protection, yet the impact has been thoroughly disappointing.

Environmentalism has a long-standing tradition in Poland. Committed environmentalists are present in many central government and local bodies, as well as among the general public. Environmental issues have been on the banners of many organisations and social groups including political parties and social and youth organisations, as well as organisations like the sixty-year-old Nature Preservation League, a League for Noise-Abatement, and a Polish Ecological Club, with widely developed international contacts. On 10 December 1988 in Krakow a first congress establishing the Polish Green 'Party' took place but after only a year of activity it was riven by personal in-fighting. None the less, in the first half of 1989 the environmentalist movement consisted of around one hundred organisations and forty less formal groupings. The Green movement will undoubtedly be strongly influenced by the rapid changes in the political and economic landscape of Poland. New laws on associations and political parties have clearly opened new perspectives but a developed multi-party structure, although much desired, was still missing from the Polish political scene in mid 1990.

Poland has a legal, institutional and economic framework of environmental protection comparable with that of many other countries, including highly developed ones. Indeed it has been often declared that the process of institution-building and of enacting fundamental environmental laws is basically complete. Yet despite this, environmental policy has clearly been ineffective. This is due mainly to two factors: insufficient enforcement and weak responsiveness in the economy towards environmental measures. Above all, the principal weakness has been the lack of integration of environmental policy within the broader framework of development strategy.

As the experience of many countries shows, successful environmental policy requires setting out precisely formulated goals which are then integrated, together with the means to achieve them, in the framework of environmental protection programmes with different time horizons.

Poland has witnessed long-standing but half-hearted attempts to integrate environmental concerns within the framework of national socio-economic planning. Environmental targets have then shared the same fate as the entire system of socio-economic plans, none of which (with the exception of the first three-year reconstruction plan of 1947–9) has been fulfilled. Plans have to be feasible, they have to be based on realistic premises and up-to-date cost-benefit calculations. No such detailed programme for environmental protection has ever been convincingly set out in Poland. The draft document prepared in 1988 by the Ministry of Environmental Protection and Natural Resources[7] was strongly criticized in many professional and political circles and a revised version was prepared in 1989. The new draft was accepted by the Economic Committee of the Council of Ministers in June 1989. Despite the political changes that occurred at around the same time (including, soon after, the emergence of a new government) that draft contains an interesting presentation of basic options for environmental policy and some of its conclusions and suggestions gained considerable professional support.

4. The June 1989 Draft Programme for Environmental Protection

The Draft National Programme for Environmental Protection of June 1989 looked ahead beyond the year 2000. It presented in a comprehensive way possibilities, principles and general methods of environmental protection and management in Poland. It addressed not only state bodies, but also the general public, as well as various social organizations. The implementation of the programme, whatever its final shape, would mean founding the whole process of socio-economic development on principles of 'eco-development'. This is the notion that social and economic goals should be harmonised with sound ecological management in the spirit of solidarity with future generations. Resource utilization, investment patterns, technological development and institutional changes are brought together to increase the possibility of meeting human needs both currently and in the future. It critically depends, however, on progress in several government policy areas aimed at:

– redirecting and rebasing socio-economic planning and spatial management on principles of eco-development,

– economic restructuring and technological change in industry and agriculture, based on ecological criteria,

– increasing general environmental awareness and responsibility,

– implementation of large investment projects in environmental control,

– successful international (both bilateral and multilateral) co-operation in coping with environmental problems.

Perhaps the most interesting contribution of the programme is its characterisation of three broad options for the socio-economic development of Poland on the verge of the next century. These are:

– to increase, as a priority, raw materials and energy production;

– to prioritize the satisfaction of consumer needs;

– to prioritize research, education and scientific spending to transform both production and consumption patterns.

It is rather easy to say what should not be done, it is much more difficult to indicate what must be done and the most complicated task of all is to say precisely how it should be done. But it is not surprising that the first option above has been rejected as the mere extension of the economic policy conducted so far and with such environmentally devastating results. The feasibility and 'affordability' of the second option may also be open to doubt. The third scenario seems to be the most promising from the viewpoint of meeting environmental requirements. If successfully implemented it could contain the process of environmental degradation in some of its dimensions before 1995 and with regard to all aspects before 2000. This would mean a tangible improvement of environmental parameters in the 'ecological hazard areas' mentioned earlier within a time horizon of twelve to fifteen years.

It is not possible here to discuss all the objectives (and difficulties) set out in the programme, but some of the more important include:

– the reduction of sulphur dioxide emission in the year 2000 by 30% as compared with the 1980 level and by a further 30% by 2010. This would allow the average ambient air concentration of SO_2 to fall below the official standard of 0.032 mg per cubic metre. The total cost of this 'desulphurization programme' was estimated at zł 740 bn in 1986 prices. Clearly, environmentally sensitive measures aimed at energy-saving and rationalization cannot be enforced where economic incentives operate defectively. Throughout the 1980s there was no effective way of increasing the profitability of coal preparation and enrichment at the enterprise level. Moreover, according to Ministry of Industry estimates the power and mining sectors cannot afford to cover more than 25% of the total desulphurization programme cost. Imported technologies are also likely to be indispensable.

– stabilization of nitrogen oxides atmospheric emission at the 1987 level by 1994, 10% reduction by 2000 and another 50% cut by 2010, so that current standards can be met.

– the programme calls for dust filtration and control devices to be generally installed by the year 2000, also for a general introduction of lead-free petrol and better water quality in all rivers.

The pollutants discharged with waste-water into rivers should be reduced by 50% by 2000 and by 2010 all effluent sources should be equipped with purification facilities. The problem of a massive increase in the salt content of the upper Vistula and Oder should be addressed and hopefully solved. All rural effluent should be treated by 2010. The progressive degradation of Baltic coastal waters should be contained by 1995. The volume of industrial waste generated and requiring storage should be lowered by 20% in 2000 and by 50% in 2010. The processing of the majority of municipal waste should be introduced by 2010. All towns should have a municipal water supply and urban sewage systems, so that 95% to 98% and 85% to 90% of the population respectively would benefit from them.

It has to be strongly emphasized that the feasibility of these tasks hinges on the development of environment-friendly reactions at every level of managerial decision-making.

The crucial importance of energy policy must be stressed in this context and some key requirements include: the modernization of combustion techniques in coal-fired power stations, improvement of fuel quality; the need for a substantial and rapid reduction of the share of the mining and metallurgy complex in industrial structure; the wider application of low-waste and clean technologies; the use of closed circuits and resource recycling in industrial processes.

The programme also argued for a regionally differentiated approach to environmental policy.

A separate part of the programme dwells on the future role of the general public in shaping environmental policy. Obviously, central government has to respect clear limitations on its own interventions. The activities of various environmentalist movements and organizations are blossoming and their political profile, in mid-1990, is far from being fully evolved.

5. Future prospects

A particularly difficult task for the future is how to secure an appropriate place for environmental concerns as economic restructuring proceeds. The 'Outline Economic Programme' of the Mazowiecki government published in October 1989 is rather optimistic in this respect, claiming that 'the switch to a market economy will force out energy and raw-material-gobbling technologies . . . first, thanks to modernization of the economic structure devastation of the environment will be reduced. Second, a state which no longer has directly to administer the economy can pursue a more effective ecological policy. Protection of the natural environment will be an integral element of the economic system and enterprises will face the real cost of using natural resources'.[8]

It should, however, be kept in mind that an integral part of systemic change will consist in a deep restructuring of property relationships and this may not inevitably lead to exclusively positive results. Extensive privatization may also carry with it some risks.

Many specific measures in the field of environmental protection and management designed as early as 1988 seem to have continued relevance also in the new political setting of late 1989, early 1990. Some of these include:

– the preparation and operation of new and tightened emission standards differentiated by region, as a base-line for the possible subsequent issuing of pollution permits;

– a ban on construction or extension of plants which could endanger the environment in areas already defined as 'ecologically threatened';

– the obligatory submission of environmental impact assessments in order to locate particular areas;

– the strict application of the ban on location of plants contested by the Minister of Environmental Protection or Minister of Public Health;

– the firm rejection of all technical projects and construction plans of all plants devoid of appropriate pollution control equipment.

The consolidation programme also suggested a range of legal and administrative actions, including:

– modification of regulations concerning personal responsibility of individuals for environmental offences;

– extension of the system of charges and fines on mobile pollution sources;

– indexation of charges and penalties in line with inflation with a substantial increase of charges and penalties for sulphur dioxide, nitrogen oxides emission and salinated waste-water discharge;

– general and firm implementation of charges and fines (including the threat of closure for severe offenders);
– greater tax preferences for producers of environmental control equipment and for firms operating in construction and assembly of environmental equipment and facilities;
– introduction of a ban on trade of environmentally harmful or hazardous products, which requires establishing a legal groundwork for licensing.

The activities outlined above were incorporated in the 'National Programme' of 1989 and according to unofficial sources the programme will now be adapted to internationally accepted standards.

The current economic and financial system of environmental protection in Poland contains preventive instruments (charges for use of environmental resources) and repressive ones (penalties). There is also a special role for incentives (preferential credit rates, tax relief and other economic and financial inducements) and subsidies from the special environmental funds established centrally and regionally. The trend towards a greater variety of anti-pollution instruments is obviously commendable and badly needed.

As was noted above the great problem appears to be the large scale of resources needed. The earlier programme was based on a total investment of zł 23 bn and this assumed national income growth in an annual range of 3.6% to 4.1% with an increase in the investment ratio to 30%.

Environmental protection and management is only one of many areas of pressing need in Poland's economic and social life. Its future depends crucially on the success of political and economic reform as well as on the response of foreign partners to urgent needs.

6. International aid

Environmental issues clearly have an international dimension. We have noted above that Poland, like many other countries, is involved in the highly undesirably international pollution 'trade'. But now the country is also keen to co-operate to clean up Europe. Fortunately, it looks also as if Western environmental aid may soon flow to Poland. At the end of 1989 the reorganized Ministry of Environmental Protection, Natural Resources and Forestry was involved in discussions with the EEC, Sweden, West Germany, the USA, Japan, the Netherlands, Denmark, Belgium, Italy, Finland, France and the World Bank.

Fourteen environmental projects with a funding bid of ECU 60 mn have been submitted to the EEC. The joint implementation and financing of a town heating scheme is being discussed with West Germany. It should serve as a model in this field, combining environmental protection with energy conservation. Some German local authorities have offered to co-operate in constructing monitoring systems for air quality as well as setting up traineeships for Polish environmental specialists in firms and research laboratories. In

December 1989 the Netherlands offered a 60 million guilder grant for the installation of exhaust gases desulphurization equipment at one of Poland's biggest power stations. Finland and Denmark have offered assistance in similar areas. The establishment of a plant for recycling municipal waste is being discussed with the Italian government. As is well known, President Bush promised $15 mn to help clean up the Kraków environment. This should allow some power plant desulphurization equipment to be installed as well as help with drinking water filtration and atmospheric monitoring systems. Japan may get involved in the desalinization of mining waste water. The World Bank may contribute $15 mn for apparatus for environmental monitoring in Kraków and Katowice. All of this adds up to assistance that is welcome and badly needed but still, in all likelihood, insufficient to repair the environmental damage caused over the last forty years.

Notes

1. Data are drawn, unless otherwise stated, from: *Ochrona Środowiska i Gospodarka Wodna 1989* (Environmental protection and water management 1989), Central Statistical Office (GUS), Warsaw, 1989; 'Conditions, dangers and environmental defence in 1988', GUS data published in *Rzeczpospolita*, 6 June 1989.
2. See J. Dziadul, 'Punkt krytyczny' (Critical point), *Polityka*, No. 15, 1988.
3. 'Narodowy Program Ochrony Środowiska' (National Programme for Environmental Protection), Warsaw, May 1989, mimeo. Attachment 1, The State of the Environment in Poland in a European Context.
4. The weak international position of Poland in this field is recorded for example in, *National Strategies and Policies for Air Pollution Abatement*, United Nations, New York, 1987, p. 21.
5. See A. Budnikowski, M. Lubiński, M. Rusiński, 'Polska a problemy ekologiczne świata' (Poland and world ecological problems), Warsaw, 1988, p. 39.
6. Biological Oxygen Demand (BOD_5) is an internationally accepted measure of pollution with biologically degradable effluent.
7. *Narodowy Program Ochrony Środowiska Przyrodniczego do roku 2010, Projekt* (Draft National Programme for Environmental Protection until 2010), Warsaw, 1988.
8. 'Outline Economic Programme', Council of Ministers, Warsaw, October 1989, p. 14.

♦ CHAPTER 5 ♦

Energy and conservation

Marek Lubiński

1. Energy policy in historical perspective

Confidence in the abundance of mineral fuels made extraction the foundation of energy policy in Poland after the Second World War. The policy-makers believed that the supply of energy did not constitute a barrier to growth and tacitly regarded it as a dependent variable of planned growth targets. In the 1960s and 1970s Polish fuel output was adjusted to the rate and structure of economic growth. Energy requirements were satisfied mainly through increases in hard coal output, which rose from 104 mn t in 1960 to a postwar record of 201 mn t in 1979, and lignite (where output increased from 9.3 mn t in 1960 to some 40 mn t towards the end of the 1970s).[1] Annual output of natural gas rose from 0.5 bn cubic metres to approximately 6.0 bn cubic metres. Domestic production of oil is insignificant and amounted to 0.2 mn t to 0.5 mn t per annum. Over the same time the country's electrical power system was developed with capacity increasing from 6,300 MW to 20,000 MW. In a number of cities and urban-industrial centres centralized heating systems were set up.

In the 1960s and early 1970s the fuel-and-energy sector's situation in Poland was fairly good. At that time Poland was a net energy exporter. Domestic demand was satisfied from home-produced fuels supplemented by oil and natural gas imported at relatively low prices from the USSR. Simultaneously the energy intensity of output fell by 2.2% per annum over 1960–77 with an income elasticity of demand for energy of 0.7. These developments diverted the attention of policy-makers from what was even then an excessive energy intensity in manufacturing, construction, housing and the municipal economy.

Consequently, the first oil shock in 1973–4 had a very limited impact on energy policy in Poland. Unlike the majority of industrialized economies Poland was not forced to take action aimed at more efficient energy utilization.

2. The energy sector in the 1980s – supply side

Poland's fuel-and-energy scene began to deteriorate at the beginning of the 1980s when it became difficult to meet national energy requirements. Of great

Table 5.1 The fuel and energy balance 1975–90 (mn t of coal equivalent)

	1975	1980	1985	1986	1987	1988	1990
Output	166.4	176.8	177.2	179.5	181.2	180.8	185.0
Imports	24.7	34.0	32.0	34.2	36.0	37.2	42.0
Exports	42.7	32.8	36.1	33.5	30.1	32.1	29.0
Stocks change	1.1	0.2	−3.1	−0.3	−0.4	2.2	–
Gross demand	147.3	177.8	176.2	180.5	187.5	183.7	198.0
Losses	46.4	55.5	56.5	56.6	51.1	49.3	63.5
Net demand	100.9	122.3	119.7	125.8	136.4	134.4	134.5

Sources: Rocznik Statystyczny, GUS, Warsaw, various years; 'Evaluation of Possibilities of Supplying the National Economy with Fuels and Energy until 2000 and, selectively, until 2020 based on Plan Provisions for 1986–1990', Ministry of Mining and Power Engineering, Warsaw, August 1987

significance was the fact that energy intensity started to increase, on average by 4.7% per annum over 1977–82. Table 5.1 presents an overview of the Polish fuel-and-energy economy in the 1975–87 period together with forecasts for 1990.

Serious tensions in the hard coal industry emerged in 1980 and 1981. They were reflected in falling output (from 201 mn t in 1979 to 193 mn t in 1980 and 163 mn t in 1981) due mainly to the suspension of work on Sundays and reduced Saturday working. Domestic demand for hard coal in 1981 was met only by cutting exports from around 40 mn t per annum to some 15 mn t. Because of payments difficulties hard-currency oil imports were also cut bringing total oil supply down from more than 16 mn t per annum in 1977–80 to 13.5 mn t in 1981. This led, of course to difficulties in satisfying demand for oil products.

The year 1982 witnessed the beginning of a recovery in Poland's fuel and energy situation. The output of coal increased (to 189.3 mn t in 1982) which made it possible to satisfy domestic needs and restore exports to 35 mn t in 1983 and 43 mn t in 1984. Thanks to the completion of the Belchatów open-cast mine lignite extraction rose from 35.5 mn t in 1981 to 57.7 mn t in 1985. On the other hand liquid fuels were still in short supply because of limited oil imports which in the years 1981–5 did not exceed 13.7 mn t per annum.

This fuel-energy recovery turned out however to be temporary, and difficulties re-emerged in 1985. The supply of hard coal, coke, natural and coke-oven gas fell short of the quantities demanded by domestic and foreign customers, and there was also a chronic shortage of oil products. These difficulties were due to growth in the economy combined with limited possibilities for increasing supply and compounded by an overall high energy intensity.

This state of affairs provided the backdrop against which the 'expansionist' 1986–90 plan was formulated. This plan assumed an inrease in hard-coal output from 191.6 mn t to 195 mn t, that is by 1.8% per annum. Nevertheless, even the achievement of such a modest increment was to prove impossible due to geological, environmental and social barriers. The most accessible coal deposits were already virtually depleted, so it was necessary to extract coal from corrugated, slant and thin, deep-lying coal beds. At present the average depth of mined coal-fields is up to 600 metres and increases by 8 to 10 metres a year. Moreover, almost 90% of coal deposits are situated in industrialized and urbanized regions in Upper Silesia where extraction, 30% of which comes from protective pillars, causes complex technical problems. The Polish coal industry is not organizationally or technologically prepared for deteriorating geological conditions.[2] Deteriorating mining conditions involve a rise in extraction costs which were estimated at 15% for the five-year period 1986–90. In 1989 extraction costs amounted to $45/t and were 50% greater than in 1975. Energy outlays in mining one ton of hard coal are estimated at present at 300 kg.[3] Environmental barriers consist, first of all, in water discharge with a daily salt content of 5,300 tons from mines to rivers. In Upper Silesia, one of the regions most heavily damaged environmentally, 75 tons of dust and 300 tons of gases are discharged every year per square km, with half of this pollution contributed by mining. Another environmental barrier is the lack of land suitable for infrastructure and for dumping sites. In 1985 'mining utilities' in the narrow sense occupied 49,000 ha (0.15% of Poland's land area) and were intended to occupy as much as 800,000 ha in 1990 (which is equivalent to 2.6% of Poland's territory).

Coal mining is a capital-intensive industry, and an increase in its capacity requires immense investment. The five-year plan for 1986–90 provided for investment outlays of zł 1.2 bn to zł 1.3 bn in the fuel-and-energy sector. This was some 43% to 45% more than the corresponding amount (in comparable prices) actually spent in the preceding five-year period and 20% to 30% more than in the 1976–80 investment plan. Taking account of the reduction in overall investment and the needs of other sectors, such an increase in outlays for fuel-and-energy was clearly impossible. But in the five year plan new investments were designed to increase capacity by some 27.5 mn t (14.3 mn t from centrally-administered projects and 13.3 mn t from enterprises' own projects).

Whatever new investment took place would clearly occur alongside falling capacities of existing mines due to resource depletion and deteriorating geological characteristics. This process was accelerated by the economic and financial system in Polish mining which was geared to the maximization of output which resulted in half of developed resources being left in the coal bed as management concentrated attention on most accessible deposits. Moreover renewed exploitation of such coal beds is usually impossible. All that was achieved was to reduce the life-span of collieries with a loss of output over 1986–90 of around 30 mn t. It was likely that maximum coal output in 1990 would not exceed 192 mn t, a rate about 2.5 mn t to 4 mn t below the 'target'. In fact 1988 output was 192 mn t while in 1989 it fell, albeit under social rather than geological pressure, to 178 mn t.

As the Belchatów mine came into operation the production of lignite rose from 35.5 mn t in 1981 to 57.7 mn t in 1985. The mine was completed in 1988 and the production of lignite is expected to remain stable at around 74 mn t to 75 mn t per annum, much in line with earlier plan provisions. A further increase of domestic lignite output will only be possible if the Knurów open-cast mine with a planned capacity of 12 mn t per annum is completed.

Oil output does not exceed 200,000 t per annum and accounts for only 1% of oil processed in Polish refineries. The output of natural gas with a high methane and nitrogen content is expected to remain stable at approximately 1.5 bn cubic metres and 6.8 bn cubic metres respectively.[4]

Council of Ministers and Parliamentary resolutions of March 1985 set out guidelines for the development of nuclear capacity up to the year 2000 in two variants ranging from 7860 MW to 9860 MW. The Żarnowiec nuclear power station, started in 1982, was to continue to be built, while in 1987 two other nuclear power stations, one the 'Warta' near Poznan and the other (without a specified location) were to be started. Both these projects have been abandoned. If the first power unit of the Żarnowiec station (capacity 465 MW) had become operational in 1990, nuclear power would still not have played a significant role in the energy balance. In any case growing social resistance is an additional obstacle to the development of nuclear power and Żarnowiec itself was abandoned in September 1990.

If the 1986–90 plan for domestic generation of fuels and energy was overoptimistic there were also clear indications that energy consumption would be higher than expected. With a growing fuel deficit during the first two years of the five-year plan foreign trade performed a balancing role. Polish exports have traditionally been dominated by hard coal, exports of which increased from 31 mn t in 1980 to a record level of 43 mn t in 1984. (This was largely thanks to a coal shortage in Western Europe as a result of the UK miners' strike.) Coal exports fell in subsequent years to 31 mn t in 1989. This was a joint effect of limited capacity and of growing pressure of domestic demand.

Deliveries of oil and oil products from the USSR usually amount to 13 mn t per annum and are unlikely to grow in view of stagnant oil production in the USSR and increased Soviet exports to the West, let alone the switch to hard currency trade within the former Comecon area. Poland's payment difficulties constitute another obstacle to greater oil imports. In 1988 oil and liquid fuel imports accounted for 35% of all imports from the USSR. Plentiful domestic resources of hard coal and lignite as well as fast growing output made the Polish authorities unaware of the long-term necessity of ensuring increased imports of fuels from the USSR. The appropriate long-term agreements which could have eased the Polish fuel balance, similar to those signed by other Comecon countries, were overlooked. For instance, oil and natural gas exports from the USSR to East Germany and Czechoslovakia are greater than for Poland whereas the population of Poland is twice as large as those of the two countries mentioned.

The gas supply situation (including imports from the Soviet Union) is more favourable. The five-year plan provided for an increase in imports from 6 bn cubic metres to 7.4 bn cubic metres and the 1990 target level of imports was already reached in 1987. It would come as no surprise if gas imports totalled as much as 8.6 bn cubic metres in 1990.

Fuel and energy have constituted a growing burden on the trade balance. In 1970 the proceeds from coal exports were twice as high as the import bill for hydrocarbon fuels. In 1975 the two were balanced but in 1980 coal and coke exports covered only 50% of the oil and natural gas import bill. The situation improved in 1987 when export revenues financed more than 70% of hydrocarbon fuel imports. These shifts were mainly due to price fluctuations. In volume terms Poland was a net energy exporter until 1985. Fuels tend to be used in Poland in an unprocessed form or as a product processed to a very limited degree. Electricity generation is also a large fuel consumer and performs a vital role in national energy requirements. The combined capacity of Polish power stations amounted to 29,038 MW in 1985. The 1986–90 plan provided for an increase in total capacity of 3,175 MW due to new investments. The actual increment, however, was unlikely to exceed 3,300 MW, and was likely to be smaller than in previous five-year plan periods. Taking account of phasing out of worn-out equipment, the net capacity increment in domestic power stations in 1985–90 was likely to be some 2,500 MW, whereas the extra amount required by domestic users, especially over winter months, was expected to be as high as 5,500 MW. Even with electricity imports from the USSR, a growing electricity deficit perhaps amounting to 2,500 MW in 1990 was expected.[5] The reality may be worse still given that per capita electricity consumption in Poland is already extremely low (Poland is sixteenth in Europe).

3. The demand side – energy consumption and intensity

The energy situation is as much influenced by demand factors as by supply. On the demand side the relationship between national income and energy consumption can be expressed by the coefficients of income elasticity of demand for energy and by energy intensity. These two magnitudes are interrelated. If the elasticity is below unity, the energy intensity diminishes, otherwise it is increasing. In the Polish economy these relationships change frequently (see Table 5.2). Despite considerable fluctuations it is noticeable that in periods of relatively fast growth, the elasticity coefficient tends to be lower. As a result, energy intensity has decreased in periods of economic recovery and has risen in periods of economic decline or stagnation.[6] This is explained by certain specific fixed energy costs, which are incurred by the economy irrespective of the level of production.

International comparisons are notoriously difficult to make due to differing methods of measuring national income, exchange rate problems and inaccuracies in converting energy calculations. Nevertheless there are solid grounds for the frequently encountered assertion that energy intensity in Poland is higher than in other Comecon states and up to four times higher than in the EEC.

Any analysis of Poland's energy management would be incomplete without specifying the causes of its high energy intensity. Losses related to processing, transport and storage (which amoun· to 30% of the energy balance) are one of

Table 5.2 Energy indicators for the national economy 1963–87

	Annual NMP growth (%)	Annual growth of energy consumption (%)	Income elasticity of demand for energy	Average annual in energy intensity (%)
1963–68	7.1	4.3	0.61	−2.5
1971–75	9.8	4.2	0.43	−5.0
1976–82	−1.8	1.3	−0.72	3.1
1983–85	5.0	2.3	0.46	−2.6
1960–85	4.4	3.5	0.79	−0.9
1986	4.9	2.4	0.49	−2.3
1987	1.9	3.9	2.05	0.9
1988	4.9	−0.2	0.04	−6.2

Source: Author's own calculations based on *Rocznik Statystyczny*, GUS, Warsaw, various years.

the major problems. About 60% of primary energy in Poland is processed into final energy through three main energy conversions, (thermal-electric, coking and refining). Conversion efficiency is measured by relating energy output to primary energy input. In Poland this ratio is 50% and turning downwards. In the EEC, on the other hand, it is around 74.2%.[7] In Western Europe per capita consumption of liquid fuels exceeds 1,500 kg; in the European Comecon countries it is 1,100 kg whereas in Poland the corresponding figure is as low as 430 kg.

The efficiency of conversion depends mainly on the quality of primary energy and is higher, the lower the share of solid fuels in the energy balance. In Poland solid fuels account for 80% of the energy balance whereas in developed countries the figure is typically only 30%.[8] Losses in the energy conversion process amount to 10 mn t of coal equivalent a year. Some of the losses are inevitable. They include power stations' own energy consumption, transmission losses, energy losses in the heat distribution network, in industrial furnaces and water heating boilers in industry and municipal services. In 1980–7 power stations' own consumption grew from 11.7 bn kWh to 14.1 bn kWh which was equivalent to almost 10% of their total output. Transmission losses have been growing systematically since 1968. In 1989 they accounted for 10.8% of production, one of the highest figures in Europe. Another factor causing losses is the low quality of the heat distribution network – heat losses are caused by improper regulation of heating systems, the poor condition of the network and their premature corrodibility. Assuming that only a half of the losses can be avoided, excessive losses measured in terms of primary energy are equal to 16 mn t of coal equivalent a year, or some 10% of global input of primary energy.

Excessive losses apart, some other reasons for high energy intensity in Poland include:

– Economic structure, the mineral resources heavy industry monoculture with, for example, low energy productivity in the steel industry as compared to, say, food processing, light industry, or electronics; also the large energy intensity of an inefficient transport system (especially motor transport) resulting from the low efficiency of internal combustion engines, the small load capacities of lorries and poor transport organization. All of this yields an excessive consumption of some 17 mn t of coal equivalent a year.

– Excessive energy intensity per unit of output, that is, products that are simply too heavy often resulting from the poor quality of materials and semi-manufactures, especially steel items. The material-and-energy intensity of the construction industry is also well known, as are obsolete, energy-intensive techniques elsewhere (for example, the use of open-hearth furnaces instead of steel-making converters). The cement industry is particularly conspicuous in this context since 'wet' instead of 'dry' cement making increases the energy input per ton of output by one third. Even if the same methods were used energy consumption in Poland would probably be higher than abroad due to mismanagement, the poor condition of equipment, underdevelopment and limited application of power engineering electronics. The end result in the steel industry for example is that production of a ton of steel in an open-hearth furnace requires an input of energy which is 17% higher than need be. Experts from the State Institute of Fuel and Energy Management found in 1985 that 'obsolete technologies contribute to the loss of 40% of energy used by Polish industry'. It is worth also noting the energy input in exported and imported goods. In the Laziska steel work the value of energy used exceeds the prices obtained in exports of the ferro-alloys produced there.[9]

– High share of primary energy in total consumption. In the process of primary fuels conversion secondary energy is produced at the expense of certain thermal losses. Nevertheless it is of higher 'quality' in the sense of its ability to do work and generate income. For example, a 2 percentage point increase in the share of electric energy required for the production of a given product involves a decrease in the total energy intensity of that product on average by more than 18%.[10]

– High energy intensity associated with residential buildings. Insulation norms in force in Poland are almost 40% less stringent than those in West Germany and 60% than those in Sweden. Even so, they are not observed. Appliances in general use such as coal-burning kitchen stoves, lamps, household appliances also tend to be relatively inefficient and energy intensive. Their joint impact on excessive consumption of energy amounts to some 25 mn t of coal equivalent a year.

– Wastage rooted in the economic system. This is a wastage which derives from technological and organizational considerations. It results first of all from production standstills and idle capacities.

The problem of excessive energy intensity was acknowledged by the authorities in the mid 1980s. This led to the 'Programme for More Efficient Utilization of Material, Fuel and Energy Resources in 1986–1990'.[11] The

Programme aimed at fuel and energy savings of 22 mn t of coal equivalent out of which 12 mn t were to be saved through centrally-administered projects and the remaining 10 mn t through enterprises' own initiatives. Better energy utilization was to have been brought about by means of:
– more effective prices. The prices for imported fuels were to be based on world prices and those for coal on production costs minus subsidies.
– better economic incentives. Enterprises were to have the equivalent of 35% energy savings exempted from taxation,
– penalties for exceeding ceilings of energy consumption,
– more attractive conditions for writing-off energy-saving investments.

However, these measures produced barely any positive results. In 1986 energy intensity of national income did fall by 2.3%, which made it possible to save some 5 mn t of coal equivalent fuel. Nevertheless, this achievement can be attributed more to a mild winter and a relatively high rate of economic growth than to the programme. The slowdown of economic growth and the severe winter of 1987 brought about an increase in energy intensity by 1.9%. In 1988 energy intensity did fall substantially (by 6.2%) but by early 1990 production was falling much faster than energy consumption. Moreover, while the energy intensity of agriculture or transport did fall consistently, the energy intensity of industry remained virtually stable. This was definitely unfavourable. First, industry – in view of its importance to the economy – plays a decisive role in total energy consumption. Second, the fall in energy intensity in agriculture merely deepens an energy backwardness in this sector of the economy. Third, the recorded fall in energy intensity in agriculture and transport was due to supply shortages rather than to more efficient usage.

Previous economic reforms in Poland exerted virtually no influence for the better on energy intensity. Until 1990 the cost-plus formula for setting prices prevailed, as did partial rationing of materials, fuels and energy as well as the subsidization of entire sectors, companies and products. Efficient fuel and energy management was not helped by low energy prices or by the lack of sufficient incentives for fuel and energy saving. The only effective savings instruments were administrative measures such as limiting supplies and rationing deliveries.

4. Possible scenarios for the 1990s

Trends in the fuel and energy balance are of key importance for the development of the Polish economy. Most forecasts prepared in the mid to late 1980s assumed that national income would increase by 3.5% to 4% per annum. Poland's annual energy requirements by the year 2000 were then estimated at some 240 mn t to 270 mn t of coal equivalent, assuming an income elasticity of demand of 0.5–0.6. It was hardly credible that supply could grow to match this demand and an energy deficit seemed inevitable. Moreover, if the income elasticity of energy demand stuck at its long-term average of 0.79, with a national income growth rate of 3.8%, the consumption of energy would amount to 282.6 mn t of coal equivalent in the year 2000. This is 106.4 mn t more than in 1985. It would generate a need for fuel-energy savings in the year 2000 of 42.6 mn t of coal equivalent assuming that supply could be expanded to 240 mn t. But this supply forecast was hugely optimistic. The planners assumed that domestic output of hard coal and lignite could be pushed to 195 mn t and 87 mn t respectively, with natural gas production up by 3 bn cubic metres and power stations' capacities up by 5,860 MW.[12] However existing constraints always made such expansion virtually impossible.

Foreign trade was viewed in those plans as an important factor equilibrating the energy balance. Oil imports were expected to reach 20 mn t in 2000, which is 5 mn t more than in 1988. Natural gas imports were to amount to 13 bn cubic metres. An agreement with the USSR provided for 9.5 bn cubic metres in 2000. An increase of this amount would involve Poland's more active engagement in the contruction of pipelines. The planned cut of coal exports accompanied by increased imports would have pushed the fuel-and-energy trade deficit from $400 mn to $1.9 bn in 2000.

Although fulfilment of this plan was always unlikely, the actual fuel-energy deficit in 2000 may amount to 20 mn t to 30 mn t of coal equivalent, (that is, around 8% to 12% of requirements). There are three ways of balancing energy demand and supply. The first of them, difficult to accept for political and social reasons, is simply to limit the rate of economic growth, adjusting it to the level set by fuel supply. The second option is to increase domestic output of fuels placing the economy under an enormous investment burden. The third, and only reasonable, solution is to utilize fuels and energy more efficiently as recommended by the World Bank in its recent study on Poland.[13] Although it may sound paradoxical, Poland's excessive energy intensity creates promising possibilities for improvement and high unit fuel consumption can be easily reduced thanks to introduction of relatively simple measures.

If energy intensity was reduced by 1.5% to 1.6% annually it would be possible to reduce fuel consumption by some 18 mn t of coal equivalent. Taking into consideration the enormous energy wastage, the task outlined above seems manageable. The experience of other countries which after two oil shocks managed to achieve zero-energy growth also points to Poland's potential for reducing energy consumption. To achieve this a number of steps are needed.

First, the reallocation of investments is of primary importance. In the past investment was concentrated mainly on increasing energy output. Given that the marginal efficiency of such investment is falling, the same outlays can bring better results if switched to energy conservation rather than extraction. Indeed some government officials have suggested that saving one ton of coal equivalent fuel requires half the outlays necessary to create the same ton. Efficiency improvements also take less time than the development of new sources of energy and are far more environmentally friendly.

Another important investment reallocation measure within the framework of the fuel-and-energy sector should be to shift priorities from production of primary energy to its processing.

Of course all this requires a change in 'energy consciousness' and overcoming the opposition of the 'coal lobby' which emerged after the Second World War. The notion that 'Poland stands on coal' made coal extraction the basic factor of post-war economic development.

The coal lobby is much weakened in the economic conditions of 1990. It was based on, and drew its strength from, state administrative and Party structures, but it also found support among lower-ranking employees in the industry. It suffered a serious blow to its standing in 1987 when the Mining Ministry was wound up and mining affairs transferred to an over-arching Industry Ministry. A Polish Coal Board was set up at the same time but in mid 1990 its future and the future of many loss-making pits looked very gloomy.[14] A huge cut in demand in the early part of 1990 prompted some lay-offs of miners and demands that the government step in to buy intervention coal stocks to keep the industry afloat.

Foreign trade has an important role to play in improving Polish energy management. It is the only way of increasing the share of hydrocarbon fuels, which are more efficient than hard coal and lignite, in overall consumption. It has already been pointed out that the balance of payment situation may limit oil imports. However, this barrier can be overcome through an export-oriented strategy and restructuring which can also contribute to more efficient energy use. But structural change needs to be far-reaching with dramatic cuts in production of highly energy-intensive items (cement and pig iron) and their substitution by imports, especially in those cases, where exports are both fuel-intensive and unprofitable.

Energy-saving investments will need the large-scale production of equipment permitting more efficient energy utilization. This includes energy-saving lights, efficient electric and diesel engines, efficient industrial boilers, and insulation materials.

The pre-condition for all this is price reform. In spite of the Law on Prices of 26 February 1982, which provided for prices for basic raw materials and production materials to be set on the basis of foreign trade prices, the official prices for hard coal and lignite were not only lower than foreign trade prices but also lower than production costs. As a result the prices of electric energy, heat, coke, coke-oven gas and city gas obtained from coal have also been too low. Because of the exceedingly low prices for primary and secondary energy it accounts only for several per cent of production costs and energy saving has been of little concern to firms.

Domestic prices were brought more in line with world prices at the end of 1989 and beginning of 1990. This resulted in a four- to fivefold increase in energy prices paid by industrial customers. It is worth noting that this still left domestic prices below world prices. Despite the increase, the share of energy in total production costs is small. It amounts to 18% in transport and communications, 4% in agriculture and 2% in industry.[15] Moreover greater economic freedom alongside considerable monopolization enables producers to shift price increases to final customers. The cost-plus pricing system and the sellers' market weaken the incentive effect of even world market energy prices.

It needs to be stressed that the difficult situation in the energy sector in Poland is ony one aspect of an ailing economic system and it is clear that overcoming the energy barrier requires changes not only in the fuel-and-energy sector but also in the entire economic system. In mid-1990 this process had begun.

Notes

1. Unless otherwise stated data are drawn from *Rocznik Statystyczny* (Statistical Yearbooks), GUS, Warsaw, various years.
2. Thin and slant coal-beds provide around 10% of total coal output but account for 45% of all coal resources. *Dariusz Sejmowy* 1985, Nos. 3 and 4.
3. See A. Spilewicz, 'Anatomia energochłonności' (An anatomy of energy intensity), *Życie Gospodarcze*, No. 26, 1986.
4. The World Bank allocated $250 mn in May 1990 to the Polish Oil and Gas Enterprise for the further development of the country's natural gas resources – Eds.
5. 'Prognoza krajowego zapotrzebowania energii i jego pokrycia do 2020 r. Bariery i uwarunkowania energetyczne' (Forecast of domestic energy requirements and supply to 2020. Barriers and determinants), Instytut Energetyki, Warsaw, November 1985.
6. For a full analysis of this see S. Albinowski, *Pułapka energetyczna gospodarki polskiej* (The Polish economy in an energy trap), KiW, Warsaw, 1988 pp. 144–52.
7. See A. Spilewicz, 'Determinaty energochłonności' (Determinants of energy intensity), *Gospodarka Planowa*, Nos. 4–5, 1986, p. 174.
8. See S. Albinowski, 'Jak mierzyć jakość energii' (How to measure energy quality), *Życie Gospodarcze*, No. 27, 1986.
9. Z. Bibrowski, ed., *Energochłonność skumulowana* (Accumulated energy intensity), PWE, Warsaw, 1983.
10. See A. Szpilewicz, *Energia a rozwój gospodarczy świata* (Energy and world economic development), PWE, Warsaw, 1982, pp. 61, 68.
11. 'Program działań na rzecz podniesienia efektywności wykorzystania zasobów materiałowych i paliwowa-energetyczna lata 1986–1990' (Programme to increase the efficiency of the utilization of material and fuel-energy resources in 1986–1990), Planning Commission and Ministry of Material and Fuel Economy, Warsaw, September 1986.
12. 'Założenia programowe zaspokojenia potrzeb gospodarki narodowej na paliwa i energie do 2000r' (Guidelines for meeting the fuel and energy requirements of the economy to 2000), Planning Commission, Mining and Energy Ministry and Chief Energy Inspectorate, Warsaw, May 1984.
13. See *Poland: Reform, Adjustment and Growth*, August 1988.
14. It is worth noting that the deficit of the hard coal industry in 1989 was $3 bn, a figure

equal to 4.2% of national income. In 1987-8 as many as 40% of Polish mines were profitable but none made a profit in 1989. It is believed by some that only a sevenfold increase in prices would bring about profitability and even then in only twenty mines. See A. Szpilewicz, 'Energetyczna panorama' (Energy panorama) in *Życie Gospodarcze*, No. 6, 1990, and T. Jeziorański, 'W biegu' (On the run), *Życie Gospodarcze*, No. 5, 1990.
15. 'Paliwowa indeksacja' (Fuel indexation), *Gazeta Bankowa*, No. 3, 1990.

◆ CHAPTER 6 ◆

Agriculture

Andrzej Kowalski

1. Introduction

Agriculture has traditionally played a prominent role in Poland's social and economic development. It has retained an important position even though the entire postwar growth strategy had an anti-agricultural character. Agriculture was undervalued, while the role of heavy industry in development was exaggerated for doctrinal reasons. None the less agriculture remained a key economic sector with, in 1988, around 14% of national income and one-third of the national work force. Moreover, more than 50% of personal income is spent on food.

Agriculture's significance is due also to non-economic factors. Despite the best efforts of the state, nearly 75% of land remains in private hands and rural communities have always been especially devoted to traditions, national culture, patriotism, work ethos and suchlike.

It is paradoxical that despite the relative 'shrinkage' of the agricultural sector over the postwar period its economic and social significance, even in the 1990s, is rising rather than falling. Indeed in Poland agricultural output has been, and remains, decisive in balancing the consumer goods market.

The role and influence of agriculture in the national economy may be analyzed along three major dimensions. First, agricultural development contributes to overall economic growth because its net product is an important element of national income. Second, agriculture influences economic growth by creating development opportunities for other industries and for international trade. Third, agriculture also influences the economy through its inter-industry impact, via the inter-sectoral transfer of resources.

2. Land, labour and capital

Economic performance and labour productivity in agriculture as in other sectors depends on input mix, input quality and intensity of factor utilization.

Production factors may be substituted (within certain limits) depending on natural, technical, economic and social conditions.

2.1. Land

Poland occupies an area of nearly 31.3 mn/ha. Of this, in 1988, farmlands accounted for 60.7% and forests (including new plantations) for 28.2%. The remaining 11% consisted of non-agricultural land or wastelands. The Polish farmland share is relatively high, as is the per capita farmland index, by comparison with other European countries. In 1988 Poland had about 0.5 ha (about 1 acre) per inhabitant: few countries in Europe have higher indices. Poland has virtually no possibility of increasing its farmland area. On the contrary, it is shrinking rather fast, in both absolute and per capita terms. Farmland area fell by about 1.5 mn/ha over the 1946-88 period. Agriculture lost over 600,000 ha in the 1970s alone. This process, combined with population growth, led to the decline of the farmland per capita index from 0.86 ha in 1946 to 0.50 ha in 1988. Given that loss of land to non-agricultural uses is an inevitable process, there is an urgent need to set out certain rules for economic land utilization, especially with regard to good farmland. The existing legislation has proved too liberal in this respect.

Poland has a rather high share of arable land (77.3%) in the farmland total. The remainder is accounted for by meadows (12.9%), pastures (8.6%) and orchards (1.2%). This structure obviously has a bearing on agricultural output, both in terms of crop and animal production.

Land quality, unfortunately, is amongst the poorest in Europe. Fertile soil is rare, and poor and medium soil account for some 70% of the total. Favourable topography does little to offset this scarcity of fertile soil. Poland's climate is intermediate, somewhat between the maritime climate of Western Europe and the continental climate of Eastern Europe. This leads to frequent weather vagaries and important changes from one year to another. The vegetation period ranges from about 200 days in eastern parts of the country to about 220 days in the west. Average annual rainfall varies from 450 mm to 650 mm.

Poland's agriculture consists of four sectors by type of ownership. Private farms own and use most of the land (72.6% in 1988) and account for most of the agricultural output. In addition to their own land, farms often cultivate state-owned land. The share of state land on long-term leases to the private sector recently stood at about 80% of its total. Small farms, founded on family labour, are dominant and farms using hired labour are rare (about 1% of all private farms). These tend to concentrate on greenhouses, vegetable production or orchards, they are usually small in terms of the area, but have high fixed and current assets.

In 1988, Poland had some 2,729,000 private farms, occupying a combined area of nearly 15 mn ha. This means of course that units tend to be small, especially in southern Poland. The average farm size (5.6 ha in 1988) is growing, but very slowly. Since 1970 the total number of farms has declined. However, structural changes are such that there is a growing share of very small farms (0.5 to 2 ha) and of big ones (15 ha plus), while the number of small and medium-sized farms is falling.

The so-called 'socialized' economy in agriculture comprises: state farms, agricultural co-operatives and Agricultural Circles' collective farms. State farms are the most important in this group. They control about 17.7% of Poland's farmlands. The remaining two socialized agricultural sectors do not manage any significant proportion of land. Agricultural Circles' collective farms[1] proved to be a complete failure and were practically dissolved in the 1980s.

2.2 Employment in Polish agriculture

Farm labour in Poland consists mostly of peasant families (on private farms). Given certain specific social and economic features of private farming, especially the combination of employment in farming with household chores, employment in agriculture can be only estimated. Labour is provided by farmers themselves, their families and others employed on these farms.

Poland's population grew from 23.6 mn in 1946 to over 37.7 mn in 1988. Over the same period the rural population fell from 16.1 mn (68% of the total) to 14.7 mn in 1988 (about 39% of the total). Even more profound changes, both in absolute and relative terms, have occurred with regard to the number of people living from agriculture. The 1950 census showed that agriculture was the principal economic activity for 11.6 mn people (47.1% of the entire population), while the same figure in 1988 was 8.8 mn (23.4% of the total). This decline in the number of people living from agriculture happened alongside a much smaller fall in the rural population as a whole. This means that a large rural population exists but is no longer involved in agriculture.

Employment in Polish agriculture remains high however, with twenty-seven full-time people per 100 ha of farmland (the calculation takes account of part-time involvement in agricultural production). None the less labour potential in agriculture has been falling during the entire postwar period, due to the permanent loss of young people to other, non-agricultural occupations. The loss of agricultural labour in the postwar period can be divided into two stages. During the first stage, the period of extensive industrial growth, a mass migration occurred, where excess labour left agriculture, usually taking up urban jobs though mostly without resettling in the cities. People often combined employment in industry with work on their land. It was industrialization on the cheap: a way of obtaining low wage labour without the need for spending on housing and the social infrastructure. The second stage, which began in the 1960s, was a period of more intensive economic growth. Migration usually involved young, educated people. The overall share of the agricultural work force in total employment fell from around 54% in 1947 to about 30% in 1988.

Population growth has been one of the dynamic elements in Poland's post-war social and economic growth. The national economy could expand never suffering from labour shortages; actually, there was labour to spare. The rapid growth of industrial employment took excess labour from agriculture, where productivity had often been next to nil. Migration made it possible to opt for labour-intensive and capital-saving technologies, using labour as the cheapest and most mobile production factor. This presented agriculture, in principle, with new possibilities for investment and land re-organization.

But can this process of labour relocation be continued? Two conflicting views exist on labour in Polish agriculture. One claims that the Polish countryside is ageing and losing its inhabitants leading to a dramatic decline in agriculture productive potential, the more so that the loss of labour is not fully compensated by capital inflow. The second maintains that there still is an excess work force on the land which makes it difficult to improve the farm structure, to increase productivity or to lower food production costs. Paradoxically both views are in a way correct. Labour surpluses and shortages coexist. On the one hand, 27.4 people are employed per 100 ha of farmland. On the other, given the inadequate development of agricultural services and equipment, more than 60% of the farms suffer from either seasonal or permanent shortages of labour. Postwar policy has eliminated traditional rural craftsmen while industry has also attracted the better skilled, offering more attractive work and living conditions than possible in the countryside. The current structure of the food economy, with its weak productive infrastructure, holds back Poland's agri-business development while the lack of social infrastructure continues to drive people out of the countryside.

2.3. *Capital*

Technical equipment in agriculture is made up of fixed assets (building, machinery, tools, pedigree stock) and current assets (fodders, fertilizers, pesticides, fungicides and suchlike). The capital/labour ratio is lower in agriculture than elsewhere in the economy due to the inadequacies of technical equipment in, and supplied to, Polish agriculture. For several decades more developed countries have seen the ratio of fixed assets to employment grow faster in agriculture than in non-agriculture sectors (largely due to rapidly declining employment in agriculture). But Poland suffered, of course, from a postwar development strategy which marginalized agriculture.

The 1980s saw a further stagnation of investment in the industries producing agricultural equipment. Nor has the internal structure of the food economy undergone any structural changes. It remained dominated by agriculture with a consistently underdeveloped processing base. For many years, out of every zł 100 spent on agricultural investment, zł 15–20 were devoted to food processing and only zł 8–9 to industries which manufacture agricultural equipment.

It is worth noting the high share of buildings in the structure of agricultural fixed assets. They account for nearly 70% of the value of non-land fixed assets. Our agriculture is clearly poorly equipped with machinery, tools, and vehicles. Of course there has been some improvement in the capital stock over the last two decades and the number of tractors in use has increased considerably. In 1950, one Polish tractor farmed 802 ha, in 1976 it had 70 ha and in 1988 a nearly West European standard of one tractor to 18 ha was reached. In animal production, however, fodder preparation, feeding and milking are barely mechanized, which necessitates large inputs of labour and – of course – lowers productivity.

The consumption of current assets in Polish agriculture is also low. Fertilizer consumption has fluctuated considerably during the 1980s but has rarely reached the pre-crisis (1979–80) peak of 193 kg of pure ingredient per hectare. In 1982–3 fertiliser application was only 170 kg/ha. It rose to 192 kg/ha in 1987 but fell in 1988 to only 176 kg/ha. The lack of possibilities to boost fertilizer production in the nearest future will no doubt constitute one of the barriers to growth of crop production. Polish agriculture also uses too little pesticides, insecticides, fungicides and weedkillers. This is clear from a comparison of the figure of 0.7 kg/ha of active agents in Poland and 4–5 kg/ha in the GDR or Czechoslovakia, and over 10 kg/ha in Denmark or the Netherlands.

Poland's balance of payments and debt problem contributed to rapid changes in fodder supply in the 1980s. Cereal and fodder imports fell from 8.9 mn t in 1982 to about 3 mn t in 1989. Domestic production was unable to compensate for such a dramatic and abrupt fall in imports. This led to a decline in the livestock population and reduced the effectiveness of animal production.

3. Agriculture output

Cuts in agricultural imports in recent years did however bring some beneficial changes in crop structure. Cereals share increased to 58.2% of crops harvested in 1988. Moreover, the share of low-yield cereals like rye and oats declined, in favour of high-yield cereals like wheat. Areas sown with cereals increased at the expense of potatoes and fodder plants. The share of potatoes in the total sown area in 1988 was 13.4%, for fodder plants it was 15.6%.

A greater proportion of land sown with cereals, beneficial changes in the structure of cereals grown and a higher productivity per hectare, combined with reduced imports, pushed up the share of domestic cereal production from 76% in 1982 to 90% in 1986–8. In 1984, cereal harvests broke the 30 q/ha (quintals/hectare) barrier for the first time in the history of Polish agriculture and remained at that level in subsequent years (31.1 q/ha in 1988).

Trends with regard to root crops are not so impressive. Potato harvests in 1988 averaged 187 q/ha and were nearly 8% lower than the 1979 record. Sugar beet yield has also been lower, 332 q/ha in 1988. Sugar content (15.6% to 16.0% in recent years) is also low. The oleiferous crop yield (two rape species are cultivated – Brassica oleifera and Brassica campestris oleifera), has varied between 23.0 q/ha and 25.5 q/ha over the 1980s.

Vegetable crops have systematically increased to nearly 6 mn t yearly.

The cold winter of 1985–6, checked positive trends in fruit production.

About 29 mn trees (mainly apple and plum) were killed by frost in 1986 and the apple crop fell to only 0.5 mn t, as compared with 1.9 mn t in the preceding year. However the crop systematically increased in the later 1980s testifying to a rapid reconstruction of the orchards.

The animal production scene is much worse. Fatstock production during the last decade was determined by the output of domestic fodders and the insufficient imports of protein components. As a result, livestock numbers fell as did animal production as a whole.

Crop production has grown much faster in the 1980s than animal production, and indeed this was the major aim of agricultural policy, since it was the only way to make up for fodder deficits when cereal imports were cut. However, the present supply of fodder and, as a consequence, animal production, would have been much higher if the crops increase had been paralleled by at least some growth in the productivity of pastures and meadows, and of potato harvests. Unfortunately, hay production has remained constant over the years, while the potato crop is falling.

Fodder shortages led to a sharp decline in meat production from 3,130,000 t in 1979 to 2,407,000 t in 1983. This slowly recovered after 1983, to reach 2,696,000 t in 1985 and 3,059,000 t in 1988.

While pig numbers have not changed much from pre-crisis times the cattle situation is serious. The downturn with regard to cattle and milk cows has persisted for more than a decade and accelerated after 1984. This decline has been accompanied by a marginal increase in lactation yield, but milk production has been falling since 1984. It may be that the decline in cattle numbers is already too serious and may have already affected the reproduction of pedigree stock.

A permanent recovery to pre-crisis levels needs a further growth in the output of domestic fodders, greater efficiency in their utilization and diffusion of better technique in animal production, in the broadest sense, including the mechanization of production and preservation of feeds, and of feeding itself.

Good results in some areas have highlighted mismatches between the storage and processing capacity of the food industry and the supply of agricultural produce, and – at the same time – have pointed to the inefficient organisation of almost all agricultural services. The situation is made still worse by the permanent shortage of nearly all types of packaging for food products. The 1986 disproportion between the increased output of agricultural commodities (6.3% compared with 1985) and the growth of processed food sales (3.6%) was a classic illustration of the underdevelopment of the food processing industry. It would of course be much more desirable if these figures were reversed but poorly developed processing potential makes it impossible. By various estimates, this underdevelopment results in losses exceeding 20% of annual food production.

4. Agriculture in Poland's new social and economic growth strategy

At the threshold of the 1990s Poland needs quickly to elaborate a new growth strategy in which the place and role of agriculture in the national economy is made clear. A growing number of people appear now to advocate that the food economy should play one of the foremost roles in this strategy.

This calls also for some care in outlining alternative strategies for agricultural development. Choosing the right growth rate for agricultural production is the crucial issue. Basically, the short-term growth rate is already determined by existing production technologies and working habits. In the longer term the room for manoeuvre is greater. A higher growth rate usually has been the Polish leaderships' preference in the postwar period. But this option tended to identify and reveal bottlenecks and other barriers which generated significant annual growth rate fluctuations. With a net production growth rate averaging 1.5% over the last three decades annual growth rates could be anywhere in the range -5.4% to $+7.6\%$, which led to frequent market disorders. Nor did attempts to maximize the growth rate lead to satisfaction of social needs. Net agricultural output often grew fast, while social satisfaction was low, because agricultural produce supply structure did not correspond to the structure of demand. But there is clearly great scope today to increase the growth rate while taking demand seriously. West European agricultural productivity is far greater than in Poland and the appropriate transfer of Western know-how could lead to a much better use of resources in Poland.

Difficult decisions must be made with regard to the land ownership structure of family farming. Nowadays, upgrading family farming is becoming the top priority. Previous structural policies aimed to consolidate existing structures and to protect all farms, even the hopelessly inefficient. These policies were rooted in primitive concepts of egalitarianism and social justice. They were social, rather than economic policies. Now, the whole system has to be realigned to higher productivity. Farming policy should be geared towards efficiency in production, while social problems should be solved by means proper to social policies. Structural transformations are crucial for the longer-term success of Polish farming. It is necessary to abolish legal and organisational barriers which limit the transfer of land to more efficient producers whatever type of ownership they may represent. It is also important that capital flows be unhindered. If agriculture can maximise its value, it must also be able to move its surplus to other areas to finance other activities.

Previous economic policies have left Polish agriculture with an enormous development gap to bridge. But it is agriculture, rather than other sectors, that can relatively quickly and with relatively low outlays diminish the gap separating us from the advanced countries.

Note

1. 'Agricultural Circles' were revived in 1956. They were partly financed by the farmers themselves and were intended to provide agricultural services. In the mid-1970s they were burdened with the additional task of cultivating land transferred to the state by ageing farmers (against pensions).

♦ CHAPTER 7 ♦

Housing

Jacek Łaszek

1. The origins of the housing crisis

The Polish housing situation at the end of the 1980s was particularly complex. On the one hand, the postwar period saw a steady, although slow, growth in housing quality. On the other hand, however, an over-centralized and bureaucratised housing policy was clearly failing to satisfy social needs. In the 1980s this was made worse by the general economic breakdown, which brought the housing crisis very much to the surface. Housing is a major social problem area in contemporary Poland, with a 1.6 mn to 1.8 mn deficit of dwellings in relation to the number of households. Standards are also much lower than people expect. The shortage of dwellings occurs mainly in big towns and affects mostly the younger generation.

Polish housing policy in the post-war period has relied heavily on the Soviet model; a 'social' policy developed in the 1920s in the Soviet Union and later adopted in other socialist countries. Its basic features were:

– The elimination of private ownership of multi-family residential buildings and of the private construction of rented accommodation. In Poland the legal basis for this was set out by government decrees in 1944–5 making it possible for the state actually to take over private houses, with the exception of smaller, one-family buildings. By 1949 private construction firms were also liquidated and replaced by state enterprises and design offices, which acted as contractors to central state investment organizations. In 1949 a decree was also passed facilitating the expropriation of land required for building;

– The elimination of the market in meeting housing needs in favour of administrative regulation. Private renting of dwellings was abolished and accommodation was allocated on the basis of set norms in square metres of usable area per person. Tenants' rights were limited, allowing the housing administration to congest dwellings. Design norms regulating construction standards were set out and implemented.[1] Rents were centrally fixed at a very low level (1% to 2% of the household budget) so that they would not be a barrier even for the poorest;

– The subordination of housing policy to the general economic policy of the state. Decisions concerning the extent and spatial distribution of housing construction were made in the central economic plan. Housing was also allocated administratively, mainly on the basis of the social 'worth' of the individual. As a consequence, the housing economy underwent far-reaching centralization and state regulation. Only rural and single family housing in small towns were excluded. But state housing policy still impinged on these sectors since their development possibilities were severely constrained by the rationing of building materials not to mention deliberate administrative hindrance.

Housing policy in Poland in the post war period has been shaped by a number of inter-related factors. First, the enormous shortage of dwellings imposed a need for regulation. Second, the allocation of dwellings was strongly linked to employment policy. Third, the logic of the economic system in the national economy (its centralization) meant also that housing investment and construction were decided centrally in the economic plan and did not depend on the demand of the population. Fourth, policy was also heavily influenced by the view prevailing in the USSR that housing should be public property and ought to have a social character.

In practice, however, policy was implemented in a far more liberal manner, with economic factors playing a growing role. This was duly reflected in housing policy developments in 1957. At around that time it was decided to accelerate housing construction by drawing on a larger share of the population's own resources in combination with new forms of state financial support. Both regional administration and state firms also benefited from new types of housing finance and were given wider possibilities to decide on the use of newly built dwellings. The so-called co-operative movement in house-building was given a boost alongside the older style state sector. Rents were also increased.

The 1957 measures appeared to work as a certain acceleration in construction became noticeable. But some difficulties were quickly revealed, especially as between the preferences of the population concerning the scale and spatial allocation of co-operative building and the preferences of the central planner. At the same time, due to the much lower rental cost of state dwellings, nobody was willing to accept co-operative housing. These contradictions were solved administratively, first by restricting access to state dwellings then by the complete liquidation of state construction. But it was not long before the housing co-operatives became highly centralized and were slotted in to the national system of economic planning. By 1970 they were simply monopoly suppliers of accommodation with no genuine co-operative character: they were little more than huge investment enterprises controlled by the central policy maker. During the 1970s other important developments also took place: the rules of 'congesting' dwellings were formally abolished and the scope of private ownership was widened as some state-owned dwellings were sold to their tenants.

On the whole though the 1970s was a bad time for housing. A heavy commitment to prefabrication and factory-based construction methods turned out to be a costly error. To make matters worse, housing investment decisions came to depend largely on the political 'strength' of local authorities, and became divorced from real social and regional needs.

Until the beginning of the 1980s construction was carried out by large centralized enterprises to which tasks and resources were administratively allocated. Decisions concerning the size and structure of buildings, technologies used, and lines for further building research were taken by the Planning Commission and Ministry of Construction. Centralized construction was matched, as noted before, by a similarly centralized investment system with projects managed by housing co-operatives which then enjoyed a monopoly over the supply of dwellings. In this system neither the construction enterprise nor the co-operative investor were interested in reducing costs. Building firms' success was evaluated mainly in terms of physical completions rather than economic results. Higher costs could easily be passed on to investors and, in turn, to the tenant or the state. As a consequence, up to the end of the 1970s the growth of contractors' building costs outpaced their input price increases by a factor of 30% to 40%, suggesting a high degree of waste.

2. Major problems in meeting housing needs

At the end of the 1970s the mounting deficiencies of housing policy coincided with a general economic crisis. In housing three distinct problem areas emerged. First, the economic condition of the construction business clearly deteriorated with falling labour productivity, growing prices and reduced activity. Second, social dissatisfaction was fuelled by the housing shortage, low standards, spatial misallocation and poor maintenance. Third, there was no real housing finance policy.

2.1. Crisis in construction

The weaknesses in housing construction observed in the 1970s continued into the next decade. The economic breakdown led to greater input shortages: construction efficiency fell further still. As GNP declined so too did the housing investment programme. Completions fell from 280,000 dwellings in the best pre-crisis year of 1978 to 185,000 to 195,000 per annum during most of the 1980s. Outlays on housing construction which, in 1982, amounted to 68% of the 1978 level were still little more than 80% of that level in the second half of the 1980s. These cuts were a fundamental though by no means singular cause of the housing crisis. Sheer malfunctioning of the housing economy was as important.

The fall and subsequent stagnation of output coincided with an abrupt increase (for demographic reasons) in the number of new households being formed. At the late 1980s pace of construction the co-operative dwelling waiting list was estimated to be twenty to thirty years long.

The structure of the construction sector did not change. It remains dominated by large, inflexible and inefficient state enterprises. During the 1980s capacity utilization at housing prefabrication plants was only around 50%, with large cost variation across different units. This was compounded by inadequate regional distribution and high transport costs. Accelerating inflation also made it virtually impossible to carry out economic calculation. While various economic reforms gave greater independence to building enterprises, their monopolistic situation often generated high profitability coupled with declining labour productivity. And despite some improvement in design, housing construction was generally low quality.

2.2. The crisis in meeting housing needs

Housing, in view of political priorities to expand industry, was treated as a competitor for scarce resources, and a barrier to growth. It was viewed as using resources but contributing little to economic development. The physical character of national economic planning meant of course that the money resources accumulated by the population had no impact on the planned volume of building activity.

Since housing was subordinated to industrialization, this meant that most dwellings were built near new workplaces. Dwellings became simply factory sleeping accommodation. As a result of this, in peak expansionist years of the 1970s, 70% of units built by housing co-operatives were distributed by non co-operative bodies. But no matter the pace of construction housing supply could not keep up with demand. Industrialization caused huge and rapid migration from villages to towns and the rate of demographic growth was also high. Poland became last in the European league Table (see Table 7.1) on numbers of

Table 7.1 Housing density in Poland and some European countries in the second half of the 1980s

Country	Year	Number of dwellings per 1000 persons
Poland	**1988**	**284**
Austria	1987	429
Bulgaria	1987	364
Czechoslovakia	1987	373
Denmark	1987	448
Norway	1986	412
GDR	1987	419
FRG	1987	448
Romania	1981	319
Hungary	1987	370

Source: *Annual Bulletin of Housing and Building Statistics for Europe 1987*, UN, New York, 1988

Table 7.2 The housing situation 1988: selected indicators

	Total	Towns	Villages
Average			
persons per room	1.01	0.96	1.10
usable area per person (m²)	17.1	16.8	17.6
Dwellings with bathroom (%)	68.9	78.9	43.0

Source: Central Statistical Office (GUS) data

dwellings per 1,000 of population. In absolute terms the record is equally poor: over 30% of households do not have their own flats.

The average number of persons per dwelling, at 3.52 in 1988, is about 20% higher than in other European countries. At the same time the average usable area of dwellings, at 59 m² in 1988, is 10% to 15% below that of other socialist countries and about 30% below West European standards. This means that the average usable area per person is 20% to 30% lower in Poland than in other socialist countries, and relative to the developed market economies the difference is even as much as 100%.

2.3. Inefficient performance of the housing economy

During the 1980s the housing system underwent little change. Municipal building which was to have a strictly social character reappeared – but its share is marginal. Instead the share and significance of companies' own building increased considerably. The latter has a quasi-statal character – it was financed mainly by investment credits or different funds and built into enterprise production costs. This house-building neglected micro- and macroeconomic rationality considerations and was certainly the most expensive type.

In the 1980s, outside the co-operative system, central regulation of rents, a high share of subsidies and a detailed administrative process in housing allocation was maintained.

As old-style building co-operatives fell down on their obligations to their members, small builting co-operatives operating outside the centralized system received a boost. This was possible thanks to a certain economic policy liberalization but the widespread rationing of building materials and land meant that, from the start, the new small co-operatives had little chance of success.

As draconian tax regulations were eased in the 1980s the private housing market received a boost. A number of factors came together to push up the free market price of property. These included ever growing personal hard currency holdings and the development, in major cities, of foreign and Polonian firms seeking premises for offices. Supply of course was also limited. In 1989 the market price of a Warsaw flat was over $400 per square metre of usable area.

Free market prices vary enormously depending on flat size, the district and the town. They can also fluctuate wildly in the short term. Property rights are still unclear and there is a lack of both financial and legal institutions enabling the housing market to function normally.

The housing economy is plagued by a number of critical defects. First, different rules for subsidizing different types of property have a strong impact on income redistribution. This has partially an inter-generational character since cheaper, highly subsidized state-owned housing and older co-operative dwellings are already occupied by the older generation and the larger, more highly subsidized flats are occupied by higher income families.[3] Second, the possibilities of flat exchange are limited. This is partly due to the difficulties of moving between different housing organizations but also due to the fact that low housing costs do not induce rationalization of consumption. On the contrary, the exchange of a large state-owned dwelling for a small co-operative flat is often connected with higher rent in a worse location. The outcome is a stronger polarization of the housing situation of the population.[4] Third, an important motivational link has been broken. There is no unambiguous road to home ownership through work and effort. Housing allocation is discretionary and the state's promise of homes for all has created a claimant attitude towards housing. The universal conviction is that the way to get a flat is through pressuring the authorities. At the same time, unsatisfied housing demand shifted to other markets especially to the cheap, highly subsidized food market and a peculiar structure of consumption, known as the food-clothing model, emerged.

In conclusion Polish housing policy, despite significant changes since the 1950s, has been dominated by a fundamental continuity. Its logic did not change – it still rejected the market mechanism, gave preference to so-called social ownership with heavy reliance on detailed administrative decision-making. Attempts at partial changes led to new difficulties and, in any case, mainly touched on the evolution of the nature of the housing investors. Before 1948 private investors predominated, giving way in the 1950s to state investors, the 1970s brought the co-operatives into pre-eminence, whereas in the 1980s the individual, and to a lesser extent the state, grew in importance.

Table 7.3 Changes in the investor structure in housing construction 1952–88 (including companies' own building for 1978 and 1988)

| | *Investors (% of total investment)* | | |
	state	co-operative	individual
1952	70.6	–	29.4
1978	18.4	55.4	26.2
1988	20.9	45.3	33.8

Source: Central Statistical Office (GUS) data

3. Directions and barriers to changes of housing policy

The housing problem in Poland has a substantial social and economic impact. In the majority of large towns much frustration exists, mostly on the part of the younger generation. Where industrial unrest breaks out the Polish experience shows that housing tends quickly to emerge as a basic issue and strikers often make housing-related demands. Recently housing has also become a main motive for emigration. It is no surprise that housing policy recently became the object of a wider discussion, during which different proposals for its reform were put forward. In general they are market-oriented.

The main factor affecting the housing economy recently was, of course, the upheaval in the overall economic and political system in Poland. The impact of this on housing was as follows:

– Changes in the ownership structure of dwellings coupled with institutional and financial transformations. Until 1990 socialized housing, that is co-operative and municipal dwellings, predominated in Polish towns. Privately-owned flats were of marginal significance. Housing was financed by low interest loans (3%) with repayment periods of up to sixty years. Accelerating inflation in the 1980s, culminating in a hyperinflation in 1989, substantially depreciated outstanding housing loans. In these circumstances the widely publicized government decision to restore positive real interest rates, combined with rumours of a possible revaluation of existing loans to their present nominal value (to contribute to balancing the state budget) provoked a mass attempt to purchase state- and co-operatively-owned flats and to repay housing loans before their maturity. It is estimated that in the last quarter of 1989 and the beginning of 1990 nearly two-thirds of co-operative flats became private property and could, in due course, enter the private market. The authorities also dissolved the Central Co-operatives Association, including housing co-operatives. It is expected in the near future that they will be split into many small genuine co-operatives. The state housing administration was dismantled and incentives to build privately, for both own use and renting, were introduced.

– Changes in housing finance regulations. The Mazowiecki government's economic policy contributed to essential shifts in sources of housing finance. Cuts in coal and energy subsidies and in direct budget support to housing maintenance led to a large increase in rents. The authorities plan to cease subsidizing the costs of housing maintenance, to introduce targeted social protection for the poorest groups (housing benefits) and to work out new rules for housing finance. The longer-term hope is to bring housing rentals to market levels (including depreciation and maintenance), to introduce property taxes on flats and to rationalize location policy. Much of the burden of these tasks will fall on local government hence the importance of the first free local elections in May 1990. Building costs also increased significantly while the government's restrictive macroeconomic policy of early 1990 also brought the construction industry up against a demand 'barrier'.

– Changes in the construction business. Higher production costs combined with the early 1990 fall in real incomes froze the demand for new dwellings and made life tough for construction firms, particularly those with highest production costs. One may expect in the near future that some of them will go out of business and some will restructure, splitting into smaller concerns.

As can be seen from the above, 1990 is distinctly a transitional period. The old mechanism ceased to work, while new ones are not yet fully operational. At present the most acute shortcomings in housing policy are the lack of real estate institutions, the absence of any efficient mechanism of social protection, of legal and institutional regulations for the property market and of clear and stable financial rules.

Western experience indicates that converting the housing economy into a profit-oriented one can be handled in a wide variety of ways. This refers both to institutions, which differ greatly from country to country, as well as to the scope for interaction between market and state regulation.

The experience in question, if applied in Poland, leaves no doubt as to the outcomes. With such a huge gap between supply and demand for dwellings there would be a hefty income redistribution and polarization of the housing situation. This would occur particularly in large towns where demographic growth and the increase in the number of new households are concentrated. It is also unlikely that there would be any acceleration in house building in those areas in view of the high costs of both land and infrastructure.

New building however is of primary importance for the improvement of the housing situation in Poland. But some political problems need to be overcome, for example, the 2 mn strong (thirty years) waiting list for co-operative housing where dwellings have been formally guaranteed. The recognition of those obligations and rights would preclude any possibility of developing other, non-co-operative housing construction.

Structural barriers to developing the housing economy include the lack of a long-term policy on building land. Much more serious, however, are the structural barriers connected with the absence of a pro-housing economic structure. In the 1980s, supplies for housing construction fell. Increased demand for building materials generated inflationary effects or shortages with no new capital inflows to the sector. Small-scale local business may help but more significant investment is needed. At present, because of the sharp slump in house-building, inputs are abundant. Nevertheless, once demand picks up the old barriers may reappear. There may also be another problem in that the housing economy, with its almost permanent 'social character' is unlikely to be a sufficiently strong competitor for resources *vis-à-vis* other sectors of the economy.

The Round Table of March 1989 agreed that housing should account for at least 7% of national income and 20% to 25% of investment outlays and that until basic needs are met public spending on housing should increase. These proportions do not differ greatly from recent levels. In 1987 the share of housing investment in total investment was 22%, and in GNP 5.6%, but this ensured only slight progress in housing standards and even this was due to the large scale of emigration.

The only real possibility for increasing housing construction lies in improving the effectiveness of the economy. Theoretically the potential is great especially, to take housing alone, because of the exceptionally large waste in all phases of the investment process. Waste starts with the highly energy-intensive production of cement through the irrationally utilized 'house factories' based on inappropriate technology and then through to badly operating building-assembly enterprises. Removing wasteful technologies requires, however, considerable investment outlays and therefore only gradual changes can be expected. The improvement of the functioning of enterprises requires in turn liquidation of giant firms and the creation of conditions for the development of new companies in a competitive environment. A reduction in excessive building demand, which outstrips the possibilities of enterprises, and of the materials supply system, is also badly needed (and seems to have happened in 1990). Developments in Poland since late 1989 give rise to a certain hope for modest success in this field. In 1990 the average size of building firms fell while their number increased and the private construction sector expanded. There may be a danger however that mass bankruptcies of state-owned enterprises may create a gap that will be difficult to fill. On the other hand, the other danger is that excessive state intervention may hamper the pace of structural adjustments.

Housing also faces other problems. It is doubtful for example whether it will be possible to maintain existing proportions in investment structure. In the years ahead one can expect growing competition from industry, connected with the need to restructure the economy.

A considerable increase in the share of the population's own resources devoted to housing would demand a drastic change in the principles of housing allocation, and hence political problems. Also on the demand side, after 1990 the currently restrained migration to towns may increase unless crucial changes occur fostering the development of agriculture and the growth of small towns. A new wave of young households will also appear.

All this will intensify pressure for house-building. At the same time housing losses, resulting from the inadequate maintenance policy of recent years, may grow.

Housing policy will undoubtedly find a balance between the strong pressure of social demand and expectations and existing supply limitations. There are bound to be institutional changes in the housing system. In general it will evolve towards a much greater use of the market mechanism though preserving, however, to a considerable degree the social character of housing with widespread administrative regulation. It is difficult to predict a considerable improvement of the housing situation in Poland in the years ahead.

Notes

1. See J. Goryński, *Standardy budowlane* (Building standards), PWT, Warsaw, 1953.
2. See A. Grabowiecka, *Wybrane czynniki zróżnicowania sytuacji mieszkaniowej w ukladzie regionalnym* (Some factors differentiating housing in a regional perspective), IKS, Warsaw, 1985.

3. See H. Kulesza, 'Zmiany w wydatkach na mieszkanie w budżetach domowych' (Changes in housing expenditures within the household budget), *Sprawy Miezkaniowe*, No. 1, 1986.
4. See J. Łaszek, 'Potrzeby i warunki mieszkaniowe ludności Warszawy w 1974 r' (The housing needs and conditions of the population in Warsaw in 1974), *IGS Bulletin*, No. 2, Warsaw, 1978.

♦ CHAPTER 8 ♦

Capital investments

Andrzej Parkola

1. Investment performance at the turn of the 1970s and 1980s

One of the most characteristic features of economic development in Poland during the 1970s was a particularly high rate of investment growth. The investment level exceeded the absorptive capacity of the national economy and became one of the main reasons for the economic crisis. In 1978, the 'engagement' of capital outlays – measured by the number of years necessary to commission all investment projects, assuming that no new projects are undertaken – amounted to 2.5 years in the economy as a whole and 2.8 years in manufacturing industry. Moreover, the investment programme had an extremely unfavourable structure. Most investments were 'green field projects', with modernization outlays taking only a marginal role. As a result, in 1978 construction took about 63% of total capital outlays. Hence, despite growing investment, an increase in the wear and tear of fixed capital assets, particularly of machinery and equipment, has taken place since 1975.

Highly capital-intensive projects, with long gestation periods, aimed at manufacturing capital goods, accounted for most investment spending. This investment structure, along with its volume, has contributed much to growing inflationary pressure. In addition, it perpetuated the traditional structure of the economy, dominated by heavy industry. The investment programme was also highly import-intensive. By the mid-1970s, imported machinery, appliances and transport equipment constituted over 50% of their total supply on the domestic market.

In the 1979–82 period, capital investment fell alongside the deep decline in national income. In 1982, the level of investments, in constant prices, was 45% below that of 1978. The slump in investment was much deeper than was true for national income as government policy aimed, as far as possible, to protect consumption.

A much reduced scale of investment activity was reflected, among others, in the freezing of a number of projects. This process began in November 1980. In 1980–2, some 1,600 investment projects were suspended. The accounting value of those investments was estimated, at 1982 prices, at 1.5 zł tn and the projects were on average, 27% completed.

Table 8.1 Capital investment in different sectors 1982 (constant prices, 1978 = 100)

Total investment	55.1
Socialized sector	50.1
Non-socialized sector	92.3
Productive investments	50.2
Non-productive investments	68.9
Industry	46.2
Construction	21.0
Agriculture	58.9
Forestry	74.5
Transport	39.4
Communication	69.7
Home trade	70.8
Municipal economy	76.0
Housing	68.6
Research and development	47.2
Education	90.0
Culture	43.6
Health care and social welfare	123.6
Sports and tourism	49.4
Outlays for construction and assembling	57.3
Outlays for machinery and equipment	47.7
Other outlays	76.2

Source: Own calculations based on data from *Rocznik Statystyczny 1986*, GUS, Warsaw, 1987, pp. 184–5

The scale of the investment slump varied in different sectors of the economy (see Tables 8.1 and 8.2). Despite an overall decline in total capital outlays of 45%, investments in the fuel-and-power sector and in industries producing consumer goods (for example the food industry) enjoyed a certain degree of protection. But the only sector in which outlays increased over the period 1970–82 was health and social welfare. Unfortunately, the efficiency of the investment process in this sphere deteriorated particularly sharply. It was reflected in an increase in the gestation period from about 44 months in 1978 to 70 months in 1982. In 1982, the average gestation period in this sector was 50% longer than the average for the national economy as a whole. As a result, increased investments did not bring about any significant improvement in either the health service or social welfare.

Table 8.2 Level of capital investment outlays in the socialized industrial sector 1982 (constant prices, 1978 = 100)

Total investments	49.5
Sector:	
Fuel and energy	77.7
Metallurgy	14.6
Electro-engineeering	39.9
Chemicals	43.4
Mineral	31.5
Wood/paper	27.6
Light	42.2
Food processing	63.6
Other industries	50.6

Source: As for Table 8.1

Different rates of investment reduction across individual sectors of the national economy brought some changes in the sectoral structure of capital outlays (see Tables 8.3 and 8.4).

The most important change was the increase in the share of 'non-productive' investments from 28.5% in 1978 to 35.6% in 1982. Moreover, it is interesting to note that the share of investments in the non-socialized sector grew from 12.6% in 1978 to 20.7% in 1982. Investments in the non-socialized sector were concentrated mainly in agriculture and housing. Among the most important reasons for the greater 'resistance' of the non-socialized sector to the crisis were stronger economic incentives, greater flexibility of usually small firms as well as rather low dependence upon supplies of investment goods, especially those imported.

The branch structure of industrial investment also changed, with a rapid increase in the share of fuel-and-power industry in total investment from 23.6% in 1978 to 40% in 1982 and an increase also in the food processing industry (the only other branch to show an increase) from 8.8% to 12.2%. The decline in other industries was especially deep in case of metallurgy, where its share fell from 16.3% in 1978 to 5.2% in 1982.

This decline in capital investment should not be unquestionably regarded as a negative phenomenon given that the 1970s investment programme was grossly over-expanded and a principal factor responsible for the crisis. Indeed, one of the main aims of government economic policy was to bring the investment front back into order. According to this line of reasoning it was necessary to adjust total investment to the capacity for its implementation. This alone should have improved to some extent the efficiency of the investment process. In the context of the cuts it became necessary to distinguish the most efficient projects, and

Table 8.3 The structure of capital investment outlay 1978, 1982 and 1988 (% share constant prices)

	1978	1982	1988
Socialized sector	87.4	79.3	82.9
Non-socialized sector	12.6	20.7	17.1
Productive	70.7	64.4	65.8
Non-productive	28.5	35.6	34.2
Industry	34.6	29.0	29.9
Construction	4.7	1.8	2.5
Agriculture	17.6	18.8	15.0
Forestry	0.5	0.7	0.6
Transport	7.4	5.3	7.4
Communication	0.6	0.7	1.0
Trade	1.8	2.3	3.0
Community services	5.2	7.2	7.5
Housing	21.3	26.5	22.6
Science & technology	0.5	0.4	0.5
Education	1.3	2.2	3.0
Cultural services	0.3	0.2	0.3
Health care & social welfare	1.1	2.4	3.0
Tourism, recreation & sports	1.1	1.0	1.3
Construction & assembling	62.6	65.1	62.2
Machinery & equipment	35.1	30.5	32.7
Other	3.2	4.4	5.1

Source: Rocznik Statystyczny, various years

this could and should have started a badly needed process of efficiency- and export-oriented restructuring.

This objective, however, was not achieved. The level of capital investment, despite its radical reduction, still exceeded the absorptive capacity of the economy. This was reflected by the increase in investment 'engagement' in the socialized sector from 2.5 years in 1978 to 3.3 in 1982. Moreover, the average gestation period in the socialized sector grew from 41.9 months in 1978 to 47.1 months in 1982. For industry it increased from 52.6 to 64.1 months. In 1982 only 59% of planned investments were completed.

Those investment projects allowed to continue were selected by administrative methods, based on very general criteria, which allowed much discretion to be exercised. The process thus became subject to strong lobbying activities. The

Table 8.4 The structure of investment outlays in socialized industry 1978, 1982 and 1987 (% share constant prices)

	1978	1982	1987
Mining	14.7	25.1	17.7
Manufacturing	85.3	74.9	82.3
Sector:			
Fuel and power	23.6	40.0	33.9
Metallurgy	16.3	5.2	6.0
Electro-engineering	24.2	21.1	25.4
Chemical	10.1	9.6	7.9
Mineral	5.2	3.6	4.1
Wood and paper	5.3	3.3	3.1
Light	4.0	3.7	5.6
Food processing	8.8	12.2	11.8
Other	1.2	1.4	2.2

Source: As for Table 8.3

best example in this respect is the share of investments in the fuel-and-power sector, where in 1982 capital 'engagement', excluding suspended projects, constituted 27.3% of the economy total and 54.4% of capital engagement in industry.

The declining efficiency of the investment process was also reflected in a further deterioration of the relation between outlays on construction and assembly and those on machinery and equipment. In 1982, the share of the former was 65.1% of all outlays (62.6% in 1978), while the share of the latter was 30.5% (35.1% in 1978).

Furthermore, the practice of passing on to firms the management of projects started originally as centrally-financed investments was hardly an aspect of genuine decentralization. The enterprises taking charge of those investments were guaranteed financial aid in the form of direct budget subsidies as well as technical credits. According to estimates made by the Consultative Economic Council in 1982 the value of those investments amounted to about 50% of all 'decentralised' investments.

To sum up, at the end of 1982 Poland continued to suffer from an over-expanded investment front, a legacy of the 1970s. The scale of continuing investments, their unfavourable composition, and administrative methods in management resulted in a further decrease of the efficiency of the investment process in comparison with 1978. It is worth mentioning here that the efficiency of the investment process in 1978 was already very unsatisfactory.

2. Investment policy after 1982

The main objectives of investment policy after 1982 were to protect the level of consumption and to increase investment efficiency. It was assumed that the rate of growth of investment during 1983–5 would be lower than the rate of growth of national income. Beyond then investment was to grow at a rate similar to the rate of growth of national income. Nevertheless, in the years 1983–8, capital investments were again over-expanded (see Table 8.5).

In 1988 total investment was 48.5% greater than in 1982 and (gross) national income was 29.4% greater. Clearly, investment outlays grew much faster than national income and faster than was assumed in national development plans.

Table 8.5 Investment growth 1983–8 (constant prices)

	1983	1984	1985	1986	1987	1988
Gross Material Product (GMP) growth rate %	6.0	5.5	3.3	4.8	2.1	4.7
1982 = 100	106.0	111.8	115.5	121.1	123.6	129.4
Total investments						
% growth	9.4	11.4	6.0	5.1	4.2	5.0
1982 = 100	109.4	121.9	129.1	135.7	141.4	148.5
Productive investments						
% growth	8.2	13.8	6.7	5.8	4.2	5.6
1982 = 100	108.2	123.1	131.4	139.0	144.8	152.9
Non-productive investments						
% growth	11.4	7.2	4.6	3.7	4.2	3.7
1982 = 100	111.4	119.4	125.9	130.6	136.1	141.1
Socialized sector						
% growth	9.6	14.1	7.6	5.9	4.4	5.4
1982 = 100	109.6	125.1	134.5	142.4	148.7	156.7
Non-socialized sector						
% growth	8.3	1.3	−1.1	1.4	3.4	3.0
1982 = 100	108.3	109.7	108.5	110.0	113.7	117.1
Construction and assembly						
% growth	11.3	9.5	3.1	3.7	2.9	4.8
1982 = 100	111.3	121.9	125.7	130.4	134.2	140.6
Machinery and equipment						
% growth	6.1	14.9	11.2	7.9	6.8	5.6
1982 = 100	106.1	121.9	135.6	146.3	156.2	164.9

Sources: As for other tables

Table 8.6 Investment 1988 (1982 = 100)

Industry	157.2
Construction	220.8
Agriculture	115.4
Forestry	124.2
Transport	217.2
Communications	234.0
Commerce	167.7
Community services	156.9
Housing	123.5
Science & technology	207.6
Education	201.3
Culture	291.6
Health care & social welfare	184.0
Tourism, recreation & sports	190.1

Source: As for other tables

The high degree of decapitalization of fixed assets, the growing technological gap as well as the lack of effective financial constraints all created strong pressure for new investment. The over-bloated investment front has been a major inflationary factor in the Polish economy.

Investment growth in individual sectors of the Polish economy was highly differentiated in the 1980s, but often with patterns quite different to those of the 1979–82 period (see Tables 8.5–8.7). In the socialized sector, capital

Table 8.7 Investment in state industry 1987 (1982 = 100)

Mining	102.2
Manufacturing Industry:	163.9
Fuel and power	122.7
Metallurgy	166.3
Electro-engineering	178.7
Chemical	119.2
Mineral	170.8
Wood and paper	141.0
Light	222.5
Food processing	162.1
Other	235.6

Source: As for other tables

investment increased in 1983–8 by 56.7% and in the non-socialized sector by 17.1%. If there was over-expansion of investment in this period it was plainly the state sector that was responsible. Investment increased more rapidly in the productive sphere than in non-productive areas.

However, with total spending on productive investment up by 52.9%, outlays on agriculture rose only by 15.4% contrary to the objectives set in central plans which prioritized the entire food sector. Its investment share fell from 23.9% in 1983 to 21.7% in 1985 and 19.9% in 1987. According to the Central Plan for 1983–5 the food sector's share in capital investments was expected to remain stable.

But in reality investment in agriculture as well as in socialized industry supplying inputs to agriculture production grew much more slowly than total spending. It was only in the socialized food processing industry that investment grew at a similar rate to that for industry as a whole. Slow growth of investment in agriculture and in industries producing for agriculture clearly jeopardizes further increase in the supply of agricultural products. At the same time, the supply of those products is still of decisive importance for domestic market equilibrium and constitutes a substantial part of exports, especially to Western countries.

Housing was also given priority in the plan and in this case plan targets were slightly surpassed. Housing and the associated subcontracting industries took over 30% of total investments. However the number of apartments built in 1983–8 was much lower than planned. The combination of substantial outlays for housing yet not yielding planned output point clearly to the low efficiency of construction firms.

The third priority area for capital investment was the fuel-and-power sector. More than 35% of all investment in state industry in the 1983–7 period was channelled to fuel-and-power. At the same time fixed investment in the electro-engineering industry, widely reckoned to be the engine for expanding exports and stimulating technical progress, amounted to less than 25% of the state industry total.

The dominance of fuel-and-power in total industrial investment resulted from a concern that a power supply shortage would threaten the Polish economy in the 1990s. But the role played by coal in generating export earnings, especially in convertible currencies, also helps to explain the pre-eminence of this sector.

Energy balance may be achieved either by investing to increase supply or by means of projects aimed at more efficient energy consumption. The former is characterised by a high capital-output ratio, long gestation periods and an extremely negative impact on the natural environment. Moreover, the fuel-and-power sector itself consumes a significant part of the power it generates. Finally, expansion of highly capital-absorptive investments in the fuel-and-power sector severely limits the economy's potential to launch energy-saving projects, indirectly contributing to high energy consumption. Energy-saving investments, on the other hand, are less capital intensive, with shorter gestation periods and usually take pressure off the environment.

The branch cross-section of industrial investment in 1983–8, the structure of new investment as well as projected undertakings shows that policy-makers were constantly pushing economically doubtful energy-generating projects at a time when resources were badly needed for efficiency-improving and export-oriented projects aimed at industrial restructuring.

The privileged position of the fuel-and-power sector results partly from its lobbying strength, but this is not the only reason. From the point of view of the government, the supply-side strategy always seemed safer. The projects were large, relatively limited, and fairly easy to monitor and control. Even if planned costs and time scales were exceeded, the government believed that future fuel and power supplies would be guaranteed. The energy-saving alternative on the other hand looked risky. Large numbers of projects would have to be carried out by many independent firms. It was also politically risky since, if it failed, extensive energy supply breakdowns could, in Poland's fraught state, cause social unrest.

Without under-estimating the risks connected with energy-saving alternatives, the negative effects of the supply-generating variant are considerable. The scale of outlays along with very long gestation periods have a highly negative impact on the domestic market. Moreover, financing investments in this branch from the budget is one of the reasons for a very high profits tax and large transfers of enterprise depreciation funds to the state budget. Firms are thus left with limited resources for expansion and even for coping with ordinary capital wear and tear. The supply-generating strategy creates burdens which the Polish economy just cannot bear in the long run.

The Central Plan for 1983–5 assumed that no investments suspended in 1980–2 would be resumed prior to 1985. This objective was not met either. The number and book value of suspended investments fell (see Table 8.8). Moreover, some projects, once suspended, were resumed and then suspended again. At the end of 1985, the Council of Ministers passed a resolution, which practically ended the process of freezing investments. According to this resolution, investments which had not already been resumed or fully stopped were to be either adopted by investors for other purposes, sold to domestic or foreign firms, given free to other socialized enterprises, or liquidated.

Table 8.8 Abandoned investments in the state sector 1983–7 (at year end)

	1983	1984	1985	1986	1987
Number	1119	863	592	427	343
Book value (mn złotys)	492.0	442.2	366.8	319.1	321.8
Engagement (% of book value)	21.5	19.7	19.1	17.0	16.8

Source: As for other tables

Another unachieved objective of the Central Plan regarding investment activity was the intention simply to reduce the number of new investments projects. Even in 1985, 34,699 investment projects were started, with a book value of zł 1,105 bn.

In general, developments concerning capital investment in the mid-1980s were highly unfavourable. The investment front was as over-expanded as ever and the target number of projects to be completed was not achieved in a single year. In 1983 actual completions were 28% below plan, in 1984 30%, in 1985 34% and in 1986 31.1%.

The engagement of investments in the socialized sector measured in years needed to complete projects (excluding suspended investments), amounted to 3.3 years in 1982, 3.7 years in 1983, 3.1 years in 1984, 3.4 years in 1985, 3.2 years in 1986 and 3.3 years in 1987. In 1978 the figure was 2.5 years.

In 1987, the average gestation period was 45.7 months, some 1.4 months less than in 1982, but 3 months longer than in 1978.

The one positive feature of the investment process was a higher rate of growth of outlays for machinery and equipment in comparison with construction and assembly. Nevertheless, the structure of investment outlays in this respect was still very unfavourable.

In 1989 investment fell and expansion that had lasted from 1983 came to an end. Socialized sector investment in 1989 (in constant prices) was 1.4% below the 1988 level. The slump resulted mainly from a tightening financial squeeze in state-owned enterprises, coupled with growing wage push pressure. The investment volume was accompanied by a parallel deterioration in investment structure. Spending on machinery and equipment fell by some 10% whereas those on construction and assembly grew by approximately 2%. As a consequence the former made up only 30% of total investment while in 1988 their share amounted to 33.3%.

3. Outlook for the 1990s

The outlook for investment will depend heavily on the impact of the economic programme of the new government, the so-called Balcerowicz programme. Other chapters have pointed out that this consists of two interlinked parts.[1] The basic objective of the first part, the stabilization programme, is to bring inflation under control. The second part, the transformation programme, is aimed at a significant increase in the efficiency of the Polish economy. This is to be brought about by establishment of a fully-fledged market mechanism, coupled with privatization of state-owned enterprises.

The stabilization programme is to work through radically restricting demand, and this is bound to create difficulties for firms. Lack of sales may mean also a diminishing propensity to invest. This is likely to be exacerbated by a dramatic reduction in tax relief, tight credit policy and loss of interest rate concessions. The new government also decided to cut centrally-financed investments as part of an attempt to balance its budget.

In general terms anti-inflationary policy tends to generate economic recession and this includes contraction in investment activity. If the stabilization programme succeeds, a fundamental economic restructuring will follow which should create an export-oriented and efficiency-driven economy in which the share of consumer industries should increase at the expense, in particular, of heavy industry.

Assuming that the economic recession can be quickly overcome, relatively high rates of economic growth might be expected for the next two to three years. If investment then begins to increase in a new market-driven context, old patterns, for example the tendency for new investment to far outweigh modernization investment, should be turned upside down. This will mean a sizeable increase of the share of machinery and equipment in overall investment. As far as the physical structure of the Polish economy is concerned a major shift in favour of consumer and engineering industry should occur, with traditional sectors like fuel-and-power and heavy industry in decline. This transformation should be facilitated by an emerging capital market which will reallocate productive factors and channel them, at long last, towards more efficient uses.

Note

1. See especially Chapter 3, by Dariusz Rosati.

◆ CHAPTER 9 ◆

Prices, incomes and the consumer market

Marian Górski

1. General remarks

This chapter considers trends in the level and structure of consumer prices and incomes against the background of the consumer market situation in Poland in the period 1978–89. We also give an initial comment on developments in 1990 and beyond.

It is useful, to start with, to discuss concepts which can be used to analyze disequilibrium in socialist economies. 'Disequilibrium' refers to the market condition when supply does not equal demand. Using the terminology of equilibrium-based economics[1] this is simply a case of markets failing to clear and in Kornai's[2] anti-equilibrium economics it is equivalent to shortage.

We confine the analysis here to disequilibrium on consumer markets only. Permanent disequilibrium states on these markets lead to some well-known phenomena: queuing, forced savings, forced substitution, 'black' and 'grey' markets. There is not yet a single and well-formed aggregate measure of 'disequilibrium'; however Kornai has proposed a vector of disaggregated indicators. For example, for consumption goods markets he suggests, among others, time lost in queuing, the number of shops visited before a successful purchase is made, the length of queues and the relation of black market to official prices. Exploring the details of these indicators leads us away from macroeconomics, if not out of economics altogether – in its market sense at least.

Here we intend to examine disequilibrium and inflation in Poland in the 1980s from a macro viewpoint and this requires a presentation of the disequilibrium issue as a monetary phenomenon. Market disequilibrium can then best be understood as an inflation in the broad sense of something leading to decreased purchasing power of money. It is important to distinguish between suppressed inflation, which is a result of insufficient supply (money can not be spent and its purchasing power can not be used) and open inflation, when money loses its purchasing power as a result of price increases. The former may be referred to as money-balance inflation and the latter simply as price inflation.

Three main macroeconomic indicators of consumer market disequilibrium have been applied:

– *Potential Money Pressure on the Consumer Market Index (PMP)*. This is calculated as the relation between money held by the population (M2 – cash and all bank deposits in domestic currency) and annual personal expenditures. Both variables are nominal and the PMP is given in percentage points.

– *Consumer Goods Reserve Index (CGR)*. This is calculated as the relation between the stock of consumer goods held at commercial companies to the annual sales of consumer goods. Again, nominal values of both variables are used and the CGR is given in percentage points.

– *The conventional Retail Prices Index (RPI)*. This is the annual rate of growth of the prices of consumer goods and services on official markets.

The two first indicators (PMP and CGR) reflect suppressed (money-balance) inflation. They should be treated as complementary: when the PMP index points to disequilibrium from the aggregate demand side, the CGR does it from the supply side of the economy. Other things being equal the higher the PMP index and the lower the CGR index, the higher is households' involuntary liquidity with deeper shortages of consumer goods and services.

The PMP index highlights the role of money as a means of exchange and can be understood as a share of the total amount of consumer goods and services sold in a given year that can be purchased by the public using the money saved in preceding years. This index can be methodologically compared with the propensity to hold money (k) in the Cambridge equation of general equilibrium:[3]

$$k = M^{d=s} / P_c \cdot C^{d=s}$$

where $M^{d=s}$ = money market equilibrium,
P_c = average price level,
$C^{d=s}$ = consumption equilibrium.

However, in our case its significance is constrained to households' money and to demand on consumer markets. The Cambridge k as an unconstrained behavioural coefficient corresponds to the PMP index level in an equilibrium state of the market. It is very hard or even impossible to assess at what level of the PMP index personal money savings reflect the free choice of the public – their voluntary savings. In other words, it is hard to know what level of the PMP index represents equilibrium. It also holds true in the case of CGR – the second index reflecting suppressed inflation. The equilibrium value of this should be estimated taking into consideration other variables, in the first place actual price inflation and households' inflationary expectations. The last increases the propensity for current consumption and decreases the voluntary propensity to hold money.

It is a well-known fact that the Polish economy, together with other centrally-planned economies, has suffered from shortages though their intensity has varied. This is why historical data from any socialist country may be of limited use as a guide to households' voluntary behaviour. An additional difficulty is that households' liquidity in Poland has been held not only in złotys but also in foreign currencies, denominated bank deposits and in foreign bank notes. In mid-1989 the former stood at $4 bn; the value of the latter is unknown, with estimates ranging from $2 bn to $40 bn.[4]

The values of the disequilibrium indicators for the Polish economy for 1978–89 are shown in columns 5–7 of Table 9.1 and on Figure 9.1. The three segments of this chart present the combination of values of any two disequilibrium indicators for each year between 1978 and 1988. The chart does not show the 1989 situation, for two reasons: at the time of writing data for 1989 are incomplete but, more important, the rate of inflation for that year does not fit the inflation scale axis applied for all the preceding years.

Suppressed and open inflation in centrally-planned economies are considered by some economists to be substitutes.[5] Such a substitutability requires us to assume that the open inflation does not create an additional increase of money supply nor a decrease in the propensity to hold money. This substitutability between suppressed and open inflation under socialism can then be considered as a process imitating 'the inflation–unemployment trade-off' in a market economy discovered by A. W. Philips.[6] It is worth adding that the similarity between these two inter-relationships lies also in that the main obstacle to the existence of the Philips curve in a market economy and 'the suppressed–open inflation trade-off' in a centrally-planned economy can be the same, namely: inflationary expectations. The relationship between suppressed and open inflation for the Polish economy in the period 1978–88 is presented in the top right corner of Figure 9.1, which can be called a modified Philips curve for a socialist economy.

A ten-year experience of one economy gives statistical series too short to verify a general hypothesis about the relationship between suppressed and open inflation in socialist economies. However, curves presented in Figure 9.1 do not confirm a substitutional relationship between these two forms of disequilibrium in the Polish economy in the analyzed period. On the contrary, one can distinguish sub-periods when both open and suppressed inflation became more severe (1978–81, 1985–8) and a sub-period (1983–4) when both forms of disequilibrium subsided. The curves of Figure 9.1 show that a rise in the price levels under expansive monetary and fiscal policy combined with wide social protection of households and enterprises, as in 1982, do not lead to market stabilization or even to replacement suppressed by open inflation. They can only lead to an extension of disequilibrium by supplementing one form for another.

2. Empirical findings

The indicators of disequilibrium on consumer markets discussed above are analyzed below on the basis of growth of Gross Material Product (GMP) and personal money income using Polish official statistics published by the Central Statistical Office (GUS) and the National Bank (NBP). The data in Table 9.1 and the curves in Figure 9.1 point to clearly distinct sub-periods from the point of view of changes on the consumer market, namely: 1978–81, 1983–5, 1986–8 and 1989 onwards.

Table 9.1 Indicators of disequilibrium on the consumer market 1978–88 (%)

	GMP annual growth rate	Rate of growth of of personal money incomes		Disequilibrium indicators		
		current prices	constant prices	PMP	CGR	RPI
1978	4.0	8.6	0.5	45.5	23.6	8.1
1979	−1.0	9.6	2.4	47.0	22.1	7.0
1980	−4.2	9.9	0.5	48.9	19.6	9.4
1981	−9.8	31.5	4.2	57.7	12.5	21.2
1982	−9.6	65.8	−18.3	47.4	13.2	100.8
1983	5.6	22.3	1.4	43.4	14.4	22.1
1984	4.9	17.9	2.8	41.6	15.6	15.0
1985	3.8	22.3	6.9	45.8	17.3	15.1
1986	4.8	20.1	2.4	47.4	17.0	17.7
1987	2.0	26.7	1.4	41.0	16.5	25.2
1988	4.6	84.1	13.8	37.0	13.6	60.2
1989	−2.2	395.0	10.0	20.0	11.5	360.0
1990	−2 to −3					350.0

Sources: For 1978–88 – official data, for 1989–90 – author's own estimates. *Note:* When official data for 1989 became available, after this chapter was written, they showed an annual inflation rate from 31 December 1988 to 31 December 1989 of 640% while the average annual inflation rate for 1989 was 244%, also output (GMP) was expected to decline in 1990 by around 20%.

We start our analysis in 1978 since this was the last year of positive growth of GMP before the crisis of 1980–1. From 1978 until 1983 the national income fell and the economic crisis became deeper. Up until 1978 the permanent 'state of suction' on the consumer market intensified and finally resulted in the acute shortages observed in the whole economy in 1980–2. The most convincing evidence of this is growth of the PMP index to the level of 57.7% and a drop of the CGR index to 12.5% in 1981.

It is a matter of record, not of opinion, that the worst point of the crisis in the form of suppressed inflation occurred in 1981. Moreover, from 1981 acute, suppressed inflation was accompanied by a new phenomenon: high and increasing open inflation. The rate of growth of consumer prices shot up from 7–9% in the late 1970s to over 21% in 1981 and 101% in 1982. The 1982 price shock was combined with a widespread income compensation programme financed by the state budget.

The budget-related wage supplements, as well as the growth of wages in reformed enterprises, raised nominal personal incomes by 64% in 1982. But because of price increases real personal income dropped by more than 18%. In addition prices growth of over 100% diminished the purchasing power of the money held by the public.

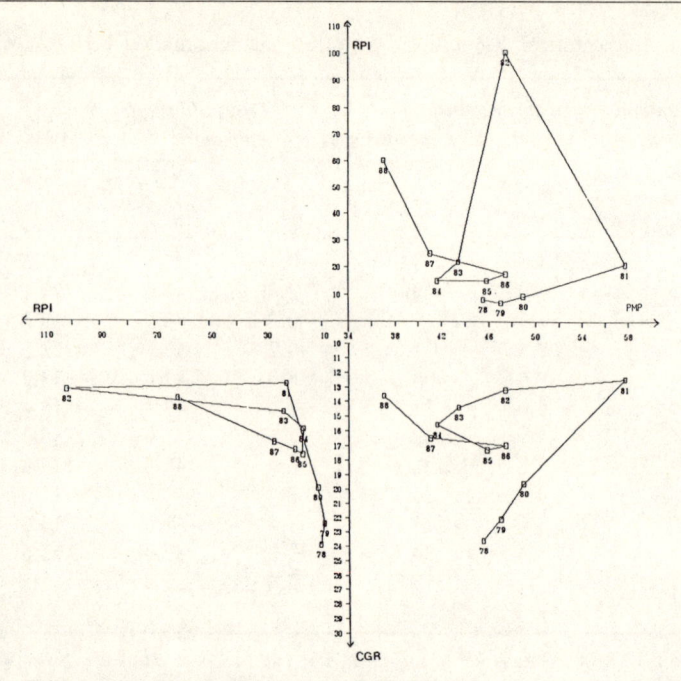

Figure 9.1 Disequilibrium on consumer market 1978–88

Personal savings rose in 1982 by 40% but the purchasing power of money savings fell by 31% over the previous year. In 1982 the PMP index reached the level of the late 1970s – more than 48% but this does not necessarily mean that levels of disequilibrium were also similar.

In macroeconomic terms, in 1982, deep, suppressed inflation was accompanied but not replaced by acute open inflation. Households and enterprises, long accustomed to relatively stable prices, administratively controlled by the state, found themselves, due to this open inflation, in a completely new economic situation.

The year 1982 was also one of economic reform and of, at least in principle, sweeping price and wage liberalization. A new Price Act established three types of prices, depending on the manner in which they were set:

– administrative prices (ceny urzędowe), set by central state agencies (the Council of Ministers, the Pricing Office, the Minister of Finance);

– controlled prices (ceny regulowane), set by the enterprises according to strict rules and a profit margin determined by the state;

– contractual or agreed prices (ceny umowne), free prices determined by enterprises according to market conditions.

In practice this classification was integrally bound with state social policy, geared to maintaining low price levels of basic necessities, such as staple foods, coal, electricity, public transport and municipal services including house rents. These prices were in the 'administrative' category and involved a high and progressively growing share of state subsidies.

Between 1983 and 1988 the various price categories accounted for the following shares of total retail sales:

	1983 (%)	1988 (%)
administrative prices	45.0	36.0
controlled prices	15.0	na
contractual prices	40.0	64.0

The above table would seem to point to gradual liberalization of the price-setting process. In reality, however, the contractual ('free') price category became substantially state-administered. A variety of controls were applied such as the requirement of pre-notifying the authorities of intended price increases and imposing ceilings on price increases for given product groups. In effect, in 1988 some form of administrative price controls applied to no less than 75% of all consumer products.

On the other hand, even enterprises under no formal price-setting constraints still continued to set prices at below market-clearing levels. This was because market imbalances offered them a variety of non-economic opportunities to exploit, while steeply progressive corporation and payroll taxes resulted in a situation where the vast part of any extra earnings from higher prices would be sucked away by the state.

In effect, a price system evolved rooted in the cost-plus formula which, given monopolistic market structure, offered an advantageous climate for an inflationary spiral to develop. Higher input costs were passed on, with an extra margin, to higher end product prices, and these in turn did not hit any 'demand barrier' among consumers.

Despite the high inflation rate, the structure of prices remained essentially unchanged over the whole period. With an aggregate price index for all consumer goods and services of 943.4 in 1988 (1980 = 100), the index for food prices was 905.8, for non-food prices 867.3 and for alcoholic beverages 1,200.[7] Polish inflation is often described as 'idle', since it yields no desirable effects whatsoever (see Kołodko (note 5)) either on price structure or on shortage. Since the early 1980s market disequilibrium in Poland has been characterised by two kinds of inflation: suppressed or money-balance inflation and open price inflation and any overall evaluation of disequilibrium must take both into consideration.

A mild though noticeable movement towards equilibrium occurred only in the short period of 1983–4. All three excess demand indicators pointed to the same conclusion: the PMP index fell to 41.6% and the RPI to 15.5% while the CGR index slowly rose to 15.6%. but it was an improvement easily made given the atrociously bad base in 1982. In 1985, however, this positive process levelled off, and for 1986 a substantial deterioration in market conditions could be observed.

This was mainly due to the lack of co-ordination between price, income and monetary policies. Adjustments in the economy's real liquidity were mainly achieved through price increases designed to lower the real value of existing nominal balances, and to some extent, through tight monetary policy designed to operate on nominal money supply. There was, however, a clear need to reduce the rate of credit expansion to enterprises and the state budget (the main factor underlying the rapid growth in the money supply). This kind of monetary policy combined with the plant managements' and government's willingness to meet workers' wage demands resulted in a rapid growth of nominal incomes of the general population.[8]

By 1988, as compared with 1978, nominal incomes of the population grew by a factor of 13, with real incomes some 20% higher. During these years a fundamental change took place in the structure of incomes, from the point of view of income sources and hence also income distribution. Polish statistics distinguish the following main sources of income:
 – earnings for labour rendered in the socialized sector;
 – social money benefits (disability and old-age pensions, social security);
 – incomes of private farmers;
 – incomes of the private business sector (outside agriculture);
 – other income, mainly interest on savings deposits held with banks and consumer credit.

The most marked growth, 27-fold, was registered for incomes in the private sector outside agriculture. There was also above-average growth (20-fold) of incomes from interest on bank deposits, and that even with negative real interest rates. There was also a 20-fold increase in the money benefits paid out by the state. In this latter case the growth in aggregate incomes is connected more with increases in the number of pensions paid out (the number grew by some 50% between 1980 and 1988), rather than an increase in the amount of an average pension. Earnings in the socialized sector grew relatively more slowly (an 11-fold increase) and the same was true for private farm incomes (also up 11 times).[9]

These trends in growth rates of various income categories have significantly altered income distribution. There was faster growth of incomes of the relatively better-off segments of the population, while the less well-off fell behind. Income disparities within society widened. One should also note that a major part of private sector incomes is generated by the so-called 'parallel economy', which is quite large in Poland but has no statistical coverage, by unrequited private transfers of foreign currency from abroad, by 'private' foreign trade (which Poles were earning a somewhat notorious reputation for in 1989–90) and also by interest on foreign currency deposits held with domestic banks.

With, during the 1980s, a non-existent capital market and administrative constraints on the scope of private business activity (for example in the form of limits on the maximum number of employees), any increase in incomes of the private sector encouraged consumption. This led to a conspicuous over-consumption by richer segments of society fuelling aspirations which were simply out of reach for the rest of society.

Nevertheless, the growth of personal incomes in money terms was the major underlying inflationary factor in the 1980s. Some 13.2 percentage points of the total 22.1% inflation rate in 1983 can be attributed to excess personal income growth over the increase in labour productivity. This means that 59.8% of the 1983 inflation was 'accounted for' by excess income growth. In 1987 the significance of this factor was greater still and grew to 64.3%, with 16.3 percentage points of the 25.2% inflation rate attributed to the growth of personal incomes.[10] The impact on inflation of growth of different income categories corresponds to their share in total personal income.

Income growth between 1983 and 1986 led to a growth in money savings. In 1986 personal savings rose by 70% and pushed the relation between money stock and expenditure (PMP) up to 47.4%. It is hard, if not impossible, to assess whether the rise in savings was due to a higher propensity to save or to deepen disequilibrium on the consumer market. Economic reform may also have given a boost to svings through a link with the expansion of the private sector not to mention an increase in private foreign exchange dealing (until as recently as March 1989 this was technically illegal but since then things have radically changed as is evident from the large number of private, and perfectly legal, foreign exchange bureaux – kantor – in Polish towns and cities).

In subsequent years (1987–9) PMP dropped again, though unlike 1983–4, this was not linked with any improvement in the market situation. Indeed consumer market supply was getting progressively worse, as is evident from a drop of the CGR index from 17.0% in 1986 to 13.6% in 1988. As the real value of household money stock holdings fell, so too (due to higher inflationary expectations) did the propensity to save.

The year 1989 ushered in a new situation on the consumer market, just as in the rest of the economy and on the political scene. From the point of view of prices and incomes, 1989 was marked above all by the acceleration of price inflation, which moved Poland into the hyperinflation league. Indeed the combination of rapidly growing prices and persistent and even worsening shortages of goods left Poland with what might be called a 'hyperstagflation'. The average inflation rate of 244% for 1989 (and the December 1988 to December 1989 rate of 640%) was due mainly to an acceleration in the pace of inflation in the second half of the year. From August 1989 until the year end the monthly inflation rate averaged 34%, reaching a 54.8% peak in October. The inflation rate accelerated as subsidies for one branch after another were phased out and price controls eliminated. This process started in August 1989 with the policy of, as it was called, 'marketizing the food economy'.

Price shocks in Poland in 1989–90 were combined with sweeping political changes in the country which made the price increases publicly acceptable. There was also widespread confidence that this would not turn out to be simply another attempt to cut living standards but would instead be the preliminary phase for recovery of the Polish economy from a protracted crisis. This combination of hardships connected with 'hyperstagflation' with hopes for improvement of the market situation is what shaped the social mood and, to some extent, market behaviour in late 1989 and early 1990.

3. Prospects for the future

Hopes for economic improvements are pinned above all on the government stabilization programme drafted by a team of specialists from the Ministry of Finance and dubbed, after the Minister himself, the Balcerowicz programme. Out of the whole package of emergency measures and systemic changes, the following were applied in 1990, and are crucial for shaping the market situation in the period ahead:

– Domestic złoty convertibility. A uniform exchange rate for all actors on the Polish economic scene, including the government, the enterprise sector and households, was established from the start of 1990. The złoty was devalued by 31.5% against the $US on 1 January 1990 and the new rate set at zł 9,500 per $. This remained stable right up to the time of writing in July 1990 without any significant drawing on the złoty 'stabilisation fund' set up by leading Western nations.

– Subsidy cuts. Budget subsidies for still more sectors, above all for coal mines and the rest of the fuel-and-power industry, continue to be withdrawn. The withdrawal of the coal subsidy entailed a 600% increase in the price of coal in early January 1990.

– Positive real interest rates. Rates both on credits extended by banks to any economic agent and offered on deposits accepted by banks were to be made positive. The interest rate, fixed on a monthly basis at the start of 1990, was negative in real terms in the first two months of 1990 but became positive in March 1990.

– Control of the state budget deficit. It was forbidden to finance the state budget deficit with non-interest bearing bank credits so ending the effortless way of dealing with this problem in the past.

– Foreign trade liberalization, including elimination of the state monopoly in this area.

The long-term consequences of this policy are difficult, if not impossible, to project. This is true both on the macro economic scale and, at a micro level, for particular markets and groups in society. The effects will depend on a consistency of policy which may be less than perfect, given the still somewhat unstable political situation within Poland and in all of Central Europe.

Forecasting developments on the consumer market is particularly difficult in view of the fact that this market will have to operate in a completely new economic, social and political environment. Capital and labour markets will also start to operate. Both are complete newcomers to a socialist economy. None the less, preliminary estimates of the Finance Ministry suggest that effective implementation of the programme will generate an early 1990 inflationary surge before things improve. In the first quarter of the year, as expected, the monthly inflation rate was high and averaged 35.7%. However this disguises the fact that the rate fell sharply from month to month: in January it was 78.6%, in February 23.9% (both figures higher than expected) and in March 4.7%. The aim of the Balcerowicz programme was to bring inflation down during 1990 to 3% to 5% per month. The course of inflation will depend, however, also on hard to foresee supply effects as well as the effectiveness with which the central bank pursues a tight money policy, in this case geared to checking excessive income growth.

Some experts estimated that the programme would require a 25% reduction in real wages but in the first two months of 1990 the fall was even deeper. The average real wage in the material sphere of the economy declined by 37% compared to the same 1989 period. Consumption also fell by a significant though unknown amount.

The drop in real wages is connected – in the opinion of the programme's authors at least – with the need to address the problem of the so-called inflationary overhang, deemed to be the leading cause of market shortages. But as we have attempted to show, the ratio of the money assets of the population to spending in 1988 was hardly excessive by Polish standards and represented no real threat to market equilibrium. It is not an excessive amount of money which destabilizes the market, but rather the velocity of circulation caused by high inflation and still higher inflationary expectations. In this light, if inflationary expectations can be damped the market might be stabilized without such a deep erosion of the real value of the money stock and of real wage levels.

This outcome would also be assisted if fiscal and monetary policy measures succeeded in stimulating greater household interest in savings, in the form both of bank deposits and of other direct capital investment. The programme certainly calls for the development of a wide variety of new savings instruments including state bonds and treasury bills and stock issues by state and private enterprises, both Polish and foreign.

Implementation of the programme, particularly of the measures pertaining to international trade, may result in a substantial change in the level and structure of supply of goods on the domestic market. On the one hand exchange-rate policy could lead to higher profitability of exports and to curbing imports. This would reduce supply on the domestic market. Yet it can, and should, spur the inflow of foreign capital, and so improve domestic supply. In late 1989 and early 1990 the supply effects of the programme for 1990 alone were being projected according to several more or less plausible scenarios, of which the most pessimistic assumed a 2% to 3% decline in GMP, and the most optimistic a 3% GMP growth in 1990. Actual performance in the first months of 1990 turned out to be much worse than this. In the first quarter of 1990 the programme produced a deep recession. Output in socialized industry fell in real terms by 25% to 30% compared to the same period of 1989.

The most valuable prize the programme can win, with repercussions for the entire economy, including the consumer market, is improved labour productivity. Yet this may take some considerable time, with a phase of unavoidable contraction as the economy switches to an entirely new mode of operation. This transition period will be full of risks and dangers for Poland.

Notes

1. See B. Felderer and S. Homburg, *Macroeconomics and New Macroeconomics*, Springer-Verlag, Berlin/Heidelberg, 1987.
2. See J. Kornai, *Anti-equilibrium*, PWN, Warsaw, 1977 and *Economics of Shortage*, North-Holland, Amsterdam, 1980.
3. See M. Górski and G. Jędrzejczak, *Równowaga i stabilność w gospodarce socjalistycznej* (Equilibrium and stability in the socialist economy), PWN, Warsaw, 1987.
4. See *Stan Państwa* (The state of Poland), Centralny Urząd Planowania, Warsaw, 1989.
5. See G. Kołodko, *Reform, Stabilization Policies, and Economic Adjustment in Poland*, World Institute for Development Economics Reasearch of the United Nations University, Helsinki, January 1989.
6. See A. W. Philips, 'The Relation Between Unemployment and the Rate of Change of Money Wages in the United Kingdom, 1886–1957', *Economica*, 1958, pp. 283–99.
7. Alcohol prices were pushed up substantially in 1987 and in 1988 by 28.2% and 68.2% respectively.
8. These demands were forcefully voiced during the strike waves of 1988 and resulted in real wage and real personal income growth (13.8%) which much outpaced growth of labour productivity. Dariusz Rosati (Chapter 3) also discusses policy inconsistencies in the 1980s.
9. The fall in the aggregate level of both income categories does not mean that real wages or farmers' real earnings fell since there was a parallel decline in state sector employment (down 5% between 1978 and 1988) and migration from country to town continued.
10. These results were obtained from calculations carried out by a team headed by the author making use of the SMIP-1 Simulation Model of Demand Inflation. This model, in addition to determining the impact of income changes, allows the effect of variables linked with the changing foreign trade situation and changes in material distribution (between consumption and savings) of GMP to be identified (SMIP-1, 1987).

♦ CHAPTER 10 ♦

The banking system and monetary policy

Grzegorz T. Jędrzejczak and Krzysztof Kalicki

1. Institutional reform

In 1989 Poland embarked on its most important banking reform of the postwar era, doing away with its centralized banking system under which nearly all monetary operations in the national economy were implemented by the National Bank of Poland. The few specialized banks which existed before January 1989 had no real autonomy with respect to loans and deposits. As a major aspect of the reform, the National Bank of Poland abandoned its former functions of a credit and deposit bank for companies and households and confined itself to a central banking role. At the same time nine 'universal' banks intended to service companies and the population were created as spin-offs from the former structure of the National Bank of Poland.

1.1. Banking system reform – historical aspects

Formally speaking, the one-tier 'monobank' system became history on 1 January 1989. The truth however is that its various consequences may linger for many years to come and bear on the effectiveness of the new system. The eventual achievement of an effective two-tier structure will depend on an ability to:
  – do away with the *automatic* credit financing of companies, replacing it with an independent policy of the central bank with regard to the money supply;
  – do away with non-economic (political, sectoral and regional) criteria of loan allocation;
  – eliminate restrictions on the management of funds belonging to economic organizations;
  – overcome the dominance of the state budget over the banking sector (abandoning the *automatic* financing of state budget deficits with bank loans);
  – create money and capital markets with free interest rates;
  – follow a foreign exchange policy consistent with domestic monetary policies.
  In the early postwar period when the one-tier structure of the banking system

was introduced, accompanied by a ban on supplier's loans (non-bank loans), the aim was simply to secure full control over money and credit creation. At the same time, however, the bank was subordinated to the central planners, which meant it enjoyed no real autonomy. This was reflected in both the legal situation, through which credit plans were subservient to, and merely shadowed, material planning, and in current pressures exerted on the bank to secure the financing of selected companies and projects. Hence, the dominance of production plans led to the automatic credit financing of material processes.

Credit policy with regard to state companies was always too liberal and as time went on, it did not take account of the rapid growth of companies' own financing capabilities.

One of the main features of the one-tier banking system was that since monetary policy depended on political and planning criteria, the banking system itself became adapted to centralized, administrative methods of decision making, rather than to any market notion of monetary equilibrium. Initially, this led to a very narrow definition of money: cash held by households and other private organizations. As economic relations evolved, a broader definition of money emerged, embracing, on the one hand deposits and, on the other, the funds of companies in the state sector. Eventually, money created by loans granted to state companies found its way to households and private companies, often becoming forced savings and helping fuel the growth of a shadow economy, with prices well above the official level for both goods and foreign exchange.

The need for accelerated capital formation was the decisive factor in shaping the regulation system of the national economy in the early days. There were two ways to achieve this: the focus could be on either budget or monetary policy. In Poland, the banking system became an instrument of the implementation of the state budget and was unable to follow any autonomous monetary policy. This was reflected in the automatic (until November 1989) and interest-free financing of budget deficits by the central bank, which in effect became an auxiliary fund of the state budget.

The combination of these features of the one-tier banking system with an inconvertible currency led to the formal separation of credit and monetary policies from foreign exchange policy and from the balance of payments. This separation of domestic monetary policy from foreign payments policy and, especially, the growing contradictions between them (an expansive domestic monetary policy, opposed to a very restrictive foreign payments policy) contributed, since the mid-1960s, to increasing pressures in the economy and to growing internal disequilibrium. These pressures helped bring about a rapid increase in the balance of payments deficit in the 1970s, which was financed by foreign loans.

A tighter loan market in the later 1970s inevitably led to the surfacing of monetary disequilibrium in the form of a more rapid official and unofficial inflation. In the 1980s, the contradictions between a non-restrictive monetary policy and the achievement of a trade surplus became even more acute, leading to ever higher inflation and the collapse of monetary policy.

1.2. Central bank reform and the new role of commercial banks

The 1989 banking reform was based on the Banking Law (which set out the principles of the operation of commercial banks) and the Law on the National Bank of Poland.[1] Within the latter, the National Bank of Poland was assigned a central banking role in Poland's monetary system, performing the functions typical of central banks in Western countries. The tasks it was given include some which, due to the current organisation of the economic system, cannot be yet performed fully such as dealing in treasury securities in the capital market.

The position of the National Bank of Poland in the system of economic control is not exactly clear. On the one hand it is no doubt strengthened by the fact that its president is appointed by Parliament at the request of Poland's President. On the other hand, the mechanisms available to the Bank to finance state budget deficits remain unclear. Until recently, the financing of state budget deficits by the National Bank of Poland took the form of the automatic extension of interest-free loans to cover the state's liabilities. The first attempt to do away with this was on 30 June 1989, following a dramatic deterioration in the state's financial condition. The question of public debt service by the central bank has not been unequivocally solved either. The law says that the central bank may provide such a service but a short-term Treasury Bonds issue in October 1989 was managed without the central bank.

The new non-financing of the public debt by central bank loans (a rule of behaviour implemented as a part of the IMF-backed adjustment programme) led to dramatic worsening of the state budget in first two months of 1990. The state had then to borrow from commercial banks until, shortly after, the deficit was liquidated.

The National Bank of Poland, in the reformed system, has supervisory functions over the operation of the banking system and is equipped with instruments to regulate credit activities.

The Banking Law creates broad opportunities for the development of the banking system. First of all, it provides for and authorizes different forms of commercial bank ownership: state-owned, co-operative, mixed state-owned and co-operative, private (public limited companies) and the establishment in Poland of agencies, branches and subsidiaries of foreign banks. Second, it permits a broad range of banking activities: opening of accounts, acceptance of savings and long-term deposits, settlements, drawing and granting of loans, cheque and bill of exchange operations, acceptance and making of deposits in domestic and foreign banks, granting and acceptance of guarantees and bank guarantees, dealing in foreign exchange and trade servicing, the servicing of state loans, issuing and trade in securities, execution of orders related to the issuing of securities, safekeeping of valuable objects and securities, provision of safe deposit boxes. In 1990 it became possible to establish in Poland either new banks with a foreign share or branches of already operating foreign banks. In fact the first such bank, the American Bank in Poland, an 80% foreign joint venture, was set up in early 1990 with a capital base of $7.2 mn. It intended to function as a merchant bank, attracting foreign capital to Poland.

2. Monetary policy

2.1. Goals of monetary policy

The basic documents which traditionally set out the goals of the monetary authorities were the credit plan and the guidelines of monetary and credit policy, voted each year by Parliament.

The credit plan
The credit plan determined the desired scale of changes in the assets and liabilities of the entire banking system. Specifically, this plan set ceilings for loans granted to the various sectors of the economy (socialized, non-socialized, households, state budget, local authority budgets) and for specific loan categories (investment, working capital, personal loans). It was an integral part of the social and economic planning system and had therefore to take account of the proportions provided in other plans, especially the central annual plan figures (on the physical distribution of the national product and methods for its financing), and of the state budget (with regard to the scale and nature of the state's receipts and expenses). The credit plan was a binding document for the National Bank of Poland and it was charged with its disaggregation for execution at the level of the individual banks in the system.

Monetary and credit policy guidelines
The set of laws on monetary policy voted by Parliament in 1988 included guidelines for monetary and credit policy, which laid down fundamental monetary targets and instruments of monetary policy such as credit rates, exchange rates, loan ceilings and refinancing loans.

The 1988 legislation declared that monetary policy should help to:
– reduce economic disequilibrium and enhance the role of money in the regulation of economic processes;
– stimulate structural changes leading to a more efficient allocation and use of production factors;
– stimulate better economic performance in companies;
– promote export production by ensuring its profitability;
– further entrepreneurship in all economic sectors.

It is worth noting that similar goals were put forward also in earlier periods.

However from 1988 in order to implement these goals, the banking system was supposed to:
– ensure that money supply growth would be lower than the distributed national income growth rate in current prices;
– adhere to uniform credit policy principles with regard to all the sectors of

the economy, allocating credit simply according to most profitable end use;
- give priority in investment loans to efficient companies, which guaranteed short pay-back times;
- differentiate the volume of loans and interest rates depending on risk and profitability;
- promote projects favouring changes in the national economic structure;
- tie credit policies to individual companies' credit rating.

Defining monetary aggregates, under the conditions of permanent shortages typical of the Polish economy, is hardly as straightforward as in market economies, because some goods and foreign exchange effectively replace local currency in its functions. Too broad definitions however, might be dangerous for monetary policy. The inclusion of foreign exchange deposits in the banks, converted at the official rate, into the aggregate of money, as proposed by the IMF, might lead to various anomalies and weakness of monetary policy. Even with local and foreign currency funds remaining at constant levels, changes in exchange rates would entail automatic changes in the supply of money. Moving currencies from private turnover to foreign exchange accounts would imply, in this understanding of the M2 aggregate, an increased supply of money, even though the level of domestic foreign exchange reserves would remain unchanged. The central bank, being only an institution which issues local currency, would be responsible for the control of domestic money supply. Even a partial 'dollarization' of the money supply would imply a loss of sovereignty by the central bank with regard to monetary policy and the introduction of external (independent from the central bank) destabilising factors.

2.2. Monetary policy instruments

Formerly, the most popular instrument used to implement monetary policy was a selective credit policy, which differentiated loan availability and terms depending on economic subject (whether socialized or non-socialized) and on the project type or area (whether central investment projects or companies' own investment projects; whether industry, agriculture, housing, exports or some other sphere). The introduction of a two-tier banking system made it possible in principle to introduce monetary policy instruments of the type used in other countries. However, given the lack of money and capital markets in Poland, it has so far been impossible to use open-market operations or instruments related to securities trading (repurchase agreements, collaterals or rediscount). But from mid 1989 a wider range of monetary investment has been activated. This included credit ceilings, loan refinancing, credit rediscounting, compulsory reserves and a variety of informal pressures. We discuss each in turn.

Credit ceilings

The central bank directly controls the volume of loans granted by commercial banks to economic organizations. Loan ceilings were introduced on the basis of the credit plan for 1989 and based on expected economic growth and the rate of inflation. For 1989 this ceiling was set at 216% of the previous year's level and the actual turn-out was 210%. This approach was partly justified by companies' excess demand for loans at previously negative real interest rates but was not expected to last because it limits banks' propensity to compete and accept deposits. The lack of restrictions on the financing of state budget deficits in 1989 resulted in the failure of the ceilings to produce the desired effects: the increase in loans to the state in 1989 was 354%.

Refinancing loans
The fact that the banking reform was launched in a situation where Poland lacked monetary instruments (bills of exchange, deposit certificates) and capital instruments (bonds, shares), made it necessary for the central bank to use refinancing loans as the second instrument of credit supply control, in addition to the ceilings mentioned earlier. It was assumed that refinancing loans were to be granted in proportion to bank equity and deposits. Refinancing loans granted for central investment projects already underway and for housing were an exception. In the latter case, commercial banks were only intermediaries, following no credit policy of their own.

The interest rate on refinancing loans was set at 44% (plus 1% commission) in the first half of 1989. At the same time the central bank introduced preferential loans, where the interest rate was kept at 75% of the basic rate for housing and at 50% for agriculture. Lower interest was also available for central investment projects. The difference in the interest rate was to be subsidized from the state budget.

The banks were authorized to exceed the limit of refinancing loans by up to 4% of the agreed amounts. This was treated by the central bank as overdue loan and penalized at interest equal to 125% of the basic rate. In the second half of 1989 the basic rate jumped to 56% (August), then to 72% (October), 100% (November) and 140% (December). None the less, the cost of credit throughout the year remained far below the inflation rate and below the rate offered on deposits by many commercial banks: the real interest rate was negative. This situation put a heavy strain on refinancing loans because it became unprofitable for the banking systems to accept deposits.

Low interest rates on refinancing loans in the first half of 1989 was further compounded with restrictions on maximum deposit and lending rates commercial banks could offer. These restrictions were lifted in the second half of the year. The lack of an inter-bank money market and the volume of refinancing loans, however, produced a situation where the cost of credit remained below the inflation rate. Also, differentiation in the volume of refinancing loans and overall ceilings were hardly helpful in promoting inter-bank competition.

Rediscount credits
The introduction of bills of exchange in settlements between Polish companies enabled the National Bank to introduce rediscount (from 18 October 1989) as a form for the refinancing of commercial banks. Rediscounted bills of exchange

must meet a number of requirements:
- they must be connected to economic transactions;
- they must be signed by at least two parties;
- they must be payable within three months.

This also offers the chance to substitute refinancing loans in their present form with rediscounting or with loans backed by other securities.

Reserve requirements
The reform of the banking system also enabled the central bank to use minimum compulsory reserves as a credit policy instrument. Compulsory reserves for time and demand deposits can be set at a maximum of 30% of their volume. Reserves deposited with the central bank bear no interest.

The following percentages were required for compulsory reserves in 1989:
- 15% on demand deposits;
- 5% on time deposits;
- 10% on savings accounts payable at sight;
- 5% on time savings accounts.

Compulsory reserves do not apply to inter-bank deposits. The volume of compulsory reserves is based on the arithmetic mean of deposits at the end of the three-month period preceding the month for which the reserves are calculated. If the reserves thus calculated differ from the actual figure, then the bank bears the cost of higher interest rate on that part of the reserves which was financed with loans. This three-month delay in the calculation of reserves, in high inflation, did much to reduce the efficiency of this instrument.

It must be emphasized that the lack of co-ordination between credit and refinancing policies limited the efficiency of the instrument of minimum compulsory reserves and failed to check credit expansion.

Informal pressures
The central bank is authorized to set the desirable relationship between commercial banks' assets and liabilities in view of preserving their liquidity. As of now, there are no formal restrictions on the structure of capital and assets, but current analyses serve as the basis used by the central bank to exert pressures on commercial banks in order to improve balance sheet quality. In the case of some unusual credit requirements, for example in the purchase of agricultural produce, the central bank sometimes appeals for special treatment to be extended to some organizations. While commercial banks are not formally bound to observe these recommendations, the strong dependence on the central bank is usually enough to ensure their compliance.

It is too early to evaluate the utility of the above instruments in the implementation of monetary policy. But it did appear initially that too many instruments were being used simultaneously without proper co-ordination. As time passed a greater cautiousness and selectivity could be observed with regard to their use.

2.3. Effects of monetary policy

Monetary policy in the 1980s had to be implemented in a difficult and changing economic background which makes it difficult to take an unequivocal view on the successes and failures of policy. It can be better appraised by considering its micro- and macroeconomic effects.

Microeconomic effects

The selective granting of loans was to serve as the basic method used by the banking system to influence companies' economic performance. Credit terms were to be tougher and firms were to be subject to strong financial self-discipline. Most of all it was hoped to generate a more effective use of enterprises' own resources in financing current operations and of both company funds and loans in financing investment projects. Creditworthiness was an important criterion in this selective approach to lending.

Information compiled by the National Bank suggests that 20% of companies using bank loans had a 'permanent creditworthiness' in 1987. This figure was only 10% in 1988. These companies enjoyed preferential credit terms. At the same time, as the figures in Table 10.1 show, the number of companies with zero credit standing fell considerably between 1987 and 1988.

Table 10.1 Companies with zero credit rating 1987–88 (end year)

	State-owned	Co-operatives	Total
1987	251	381	632
1988	184	202	386

Source: *Sprawozdanie z realizacji planu kredytowego i założeń polityki pieniężno-kredytowej w 1988r* (Report on the implementation of the credit plan and of the guidelines of monetary and credit policy in 1988), National Bank, Warsaw, 1988, p. 13.

Various reasons were responsible for the decline in the number of uncreditworthy companies and the most important were accelerating inflation, which enabled inefficient companies to pass on their growing costs to customers in higher prices, and relative ease of obtaining financial assistance in the form of subventions and budget subsidies.

To a large extent, these factors supported an expansive credit policy, and helped produce a lack of consistency in monetary policy.

In the first three months of 1990 the financial situation of many firms changed radically but the impact of this on their creditworthiness is still unclear. Some estimates indicate that about 10% of Polish firms were threatened with insolvency in 1990. On the other hand it seems clear that many firms may be bargaining on an easing of the restrictiveness of credit policy.

THE BANKING SYSTEM & MONETARY POLICY 103

Macroeconomic effects

Table 10.2 provides basic data for the evaluation of the effects of monetary policy in the years 1982–9. Several elements contributed to the low efficiency of monetary policy in the 1980s. First, one must note the constraints deriving from economic policy implemented during that period. The doubling of prices at the beginning of 1982, combined with the much lower growth of personal incomes, was the most notable financial event in that period.

Initially, this operation produced a drop in real wages and the depreciation of

Table 10.2 Changes in selected parameters illustrating monetary policy 1982–9 (% changes)

	1982	1983	1984	1985	1986	1987	1988	1989
GMP[a]	108.3	23.6	22.4	20.2	23.9	31.4	76.8	312.0
GMP[b]	(4.8)	6.0	5.5	3.3	4.8	2.1	4.7	(5.0)
GMP deflator	118.8	16.6	16.0	16.4	18.2	28.7	68.9	334.0
Personal incomes	64.9	23.0	18.3	23.3	19.2	26.0	84.4	na
Prices	104.5	21.4	14.8	15.0	17.5	25.3	61.3	343.0
M1	38.9	10.9	15.5	20.4	21.8	25.9	59.0	96.8
M2	38.0	17.5	19.8	19.9	25.4	22.8	51.6	124.9
M2 (IMF)	38.6	17.4	21.0	22.1	28.9	32.1	61.1	316.5
Total loans	16.2	14.9	12.0	18.1	16.7	17.7	43.2	86.2
Loans for state budget	22.5	56.2	22.0	24.3	2.0	31.8	64.3	254.0
Nominal interest rates:[c]								
State sector	6.0	6.0	6.0	6.0	6.0	6.0	10.0	87.0
Private sector	10.0	10.0	10.0	10.0	10.0	10.0	25.0	87.0
Real interest rates:								
State sector	(52.3)	(9.3)	(9.4)	(8.7)	(11.0)	(16.5)	(35.2)	(56.8)
Private sector	(50.0)	(5.8)	(6.0)	(5.3)	(7.6)	(13.3)	(26.3)	(56.8)
Ratio of								
M2/GMP[d]	52.8	50.2	49.0	48.8	49.0	46.5	39.7	21.7
M2/GMP[e]	54.8	52.1	51.4	52.1	53.8	54.9	49.8	50.5

Notes: values in parentheses are negative, 1989 data are preliminary; a – current prices; b – constant prices; c – interest rates on 1-year deposits; d – excluding foreign exchange deposits; e – including foreign exchange deposits converted at official exchange rates as recommended by the IMF.

Sources: Rocznik Statystyczny, GUS, Warsaw, various years, National Bank of Poland.

household savings and company funds. The aim was to achieve global equilibrium and to impose hard budget constraints on economic organizations. The price shock, however, failed to achieve equilibrium in 1982, and in subsequent years it produced a growth in households and companies' revenues which was higher than real GMP growth, which led to two-digit open inflation and boosted repressed inflation.[2]

Looking for the causes of the above developments in the province of monetary policy, one must first note a too rapid growth of the money supply. Interest-free loans for the financing of budget deficits have been the main source of excessive money growth. The years 1986 and 1988 excepted, the growth rate of these loans was greater than the value of the GMP deflator.

A progressive 'dollarization' of the Polish economy was another deficiency of Polish monetary policy in the 1980s. Everyday microeconomic observations are corroborated by macroeconomic data. There has been a systematic decline in the ratio of the M2 aggregate (without foreign exchange deposits) to GMP, accompanied by a nearly constant relationship between M2 with foreign exchange deposits to GMP. Considering that there were additional sources of foreign exchange used for transaction purposes but not included in these calculations, and that the exchange rate adopted for the conversion of foreign exchange deposits was too low, then the decline in importance of the domestic currency in transactions becomes obvious. This 'dollarization' appeared all the more dangerous because of the vicious circle it threatened: the enhanced importance of foreign currencies results from ineffective monetary policies in the past, yet at the same time, it severely undermines the chances of introducing effective policies in the future. The experiences of internal convertibility introduced in 1990 are too short to change public attitudes to domestic and foreign currencies as means of transactions in specific markets. Another deficiency of monetary policy lay in the persistence of negative real interest rates throughout the whole of the 1980s.

Eventually one comes to the question regarding the factors underlying the clear deterioration of market equilibrium (higher inflation) in a situation when in 1988 the growth of money supply was lower than GMP growth in current prices. Two factors may have played a particularly important role:

– the year 1988 saw the cumulation of price increases overdue from the 1985–7 period;

– anticipated price increases may have been overestimated bringing about a decline in the demand for local currency and a flight from the złoty into convertible currencies and goods.

The fragmentary data provided in Table 10.3 show initial macro-monetary results of 1990.

3. Banking system and monetary policy in transition

There is no doubt that the banking system and monetary policy will be one of the crucial and, at the same time, most vulnerable elements of the radical

Table 10.3 Changes in selected parameters illustrating monetary policy, first quarter of 1990 compared to the end of 1989 (%)

Variable	Jan.–March
Retail prices	115.1
Cost of living	145.6
Personal income	95.5
Loans for non-monetary sphere	62.1
Loans for households	90.0
Loans for the economy	55.4
M2 (IMF) Aggregate	15.4
M2 Aggregate	96.9
Nominal interest on 1-year deposits (monthly):	36%; 20%; 10%.

Source: GUS Preliminary Report on Socio-Economic Situation in 1989, Warsaw, February 1990.

transformations of the Polish economy. The elements mentioned below will no doubt play a major role.

– The establishment of institutional and real conditions for the separation of the competencies and operations of the central bank from those of the government. This must consist in the elimination of the financing of state budget deficits with bank loans. The late 1980s saw some move in that direction and in 1990 it seemed to become a reality. What is needed here is the creation of financial instruments enhancing the autonomy of the monetary authorities. This calls for the introduction of securities as a means of financing budget expenses. Such securities, subject to the creation of an appropriate market, would be a material foundation for the implementation of monetary policy through open-market operations.

– The operations of commercial banks in monetary and capital markets (primary and secondary). This is connected with the broadly drawn programme for the privatization of the Polish economy and would require the creation of a broad network of banks with both private and foreign capital participation. These banks should operate both as broker/dealers and as investment banks. The need for specialized banks capable of servicing the securities exchange is a question apart. All this will call for major shifts in the organization of the banking system (making it comparable to Western systems) and a complete change in banking attitudes – from a quasi-administrative rationing of loans towards profit-making operations. From this point of view the shortage of properly trained staff is clearly visible. In 1989–90 some potentially important developments took place in this field with the support of the UK government 'Know-How Fund' as well as a French initiative to set up a leading banking school in Katowice.

– A far-reaching deregulation of the banking system is required, concerning both interest rates and the scope of admissible bank operations. This seems bound to lead to both greater competitiveness and positive real interest rates.

– There are plans to base monetary policies in the 1990s on money supply targets rather than on credit plans. The implementation of such a monetary policy would call for a very precise definition of monetary aggregates controlled and influenced by the central bank and demand further research on the money multiplier in the post-centrally-planned economy.

Notes

1. See *Dziennik Ustaw*, No. 4, 10 February 1989 items 21 and 22.
2. See also comments on macro-disequilibrium in Górski, chapter 9.

♦ CHAPTER 11 ♦

Privatization and the private sector

Grzegorz T. Jędrzejczak

1. The private sector in the national economy

1.1. The concept of the private sector

In the Polish economy, the domain of the private sector is not clearly marked. Outside a visible centre of owner-managed and small private limited companies we have a grey sphere which, from the point of view of ownership, is diversified. This is the result of a long period of political and fiscal discrimination against private ownership and has had the following practical consequences:
 – a significant part of the private sector was pushed towards a shadow or even black economy;
 – co-operatives lost their original character because of tight bureaucratic control;
 – in the 1980s it became possible to 'mix' state and private (including foreign) capital in the form of companies as well as through long-term leasing of state assets to individuals and private companies.

The state-owned enterprise is the basic unit in the national economy. Separate laws regulate the legal and financial statutes of the state enterprise, guaranteeing far-reaching organizational and financial independence. The state's interests, within the state enterprise, are represented by the general manager as well as by the system and structures of employee self-management. The interests of the state, as enterprise owner, are represented by the firm's so called 'founding body', which consists usually of a number of representatives of various ministries and local authorities. The enterprise has at its disposal all of its assets, and is able to sell them to private parties as well as to invest them in other companies. It can not, however, without the approval of the founding body, liquidate itself or transform itself into a joint stock company.

Production co-operatives are also indistinguishable, to all intents and purposes, from state enterprises in a strict sense. The activities of the co-operatives are strictly controlled by the state and they have entered the national planning system in the usual (directive) way.

1.2. The scale of private and public ownership in the national economy

There are problems in clearly distinguishing private and public ownership which undoubtedly influence the possibility of precisely evaluating the scale of private economic activity. The main methodological problems include:
– distorted price relations, particularly important when the valuation of assets takes place,
– the existence of an important shadow economy which some estimates suggest makes up as much as 15% of Gross Material Product (GMP).[1]

Table 11.1 Public and private ownership in the national economy (% share at end 1988)

Sectors of national economy		Total	Forms of ownership	
			Public (State owned + co-operatives)	Private
Economy, total	A	100	81.9	18.1
	B	100	65.5	34.5
	C	100	70.6	29.4
Industry	A	100	93.6	6.4
	B	100	88.3	11.7
	C	100	97.9	2.1
Agriculture	A	100	29.4	70.6
	B	100	21.1	78.9
	C	100	34.3	65.7
Construction	A	100	79.2	20.8
	B	100	79.3	20.7
	C	100	90.2	9.8
Transport	A	100	na	na
	B	100	95.9	4.1
	C	100	99.1	0.9
Commerce	A	100	na	na
	B	100	93.9	6.1
	C	100	96.8	5.2

Symbols: A – Gross Material Product (GMP), 1988; B – Average employment in 1988; C – Net value of fixed assets (current prices) at the end of 1988.
Source: *Rocznik Statystyczny 1989*, GUS, Warsaw.

Table 11.2 Number of firms and average employment in private and public industry (end 1988)

	No. of firms	Average employment
Private industry	231,295	3
Public industry:		
Total of which	5,823	713
state-owned	3,177	1,132
co-operatives	2,400	219

Source: Rocznik Statystyczny, 1989.

Table 11.3 Distribution of public enterprises in industry according to employment (end 1988)

Industry	Firms (no.)	Av. empl.	% of firms with employment:							
			Less than 50	51–100	101–200	201–500	501–1000	1001–2000	2001–5000	Over 5000
Total	5,823	713	8.2	8.7	19.9	30.2	15.4	10.2	5.5	1.9
State firms	3,177	1,132	3.7	4.7	9.4	26.3	23.9	18.3	10.1	3.6
Co-operatives	2,400	219	8.3	14.1	34.7	36.9	5.5	0.4	0.1	–
Industry:										
Coal mining	95	5,054	1.0	–	9.5	6.3	–	4.2	30.5	48.5
Energy generation	90	1,337	2.2	–	6.7	15.6	17.8	36.7	19.9	1.1
Metallurgy	73	2,907	4.1	5.5	2.7	19.2	10.9	13.7	28.8	15.1
Engineering	611	714	11.0	6.4	17.7	28.5	18.0	11.8	5.5	1.1
Precision instruments	155	523	20.7	9.0	17.4	27.1	11.0	8.4	5.8	0.6
Means of transport	295	1,141	9.2	6.4	13.6	27.8	21.3	10.5	6.1	5.1
Electrotechnology and electronic	300	830	12.0	4.7	10.0	31.6	20.7	9.0	9.3	2.7
Chemical	402	652	8.0	6.7	24.1	33.1	12.2	8.0	5.2	2.7
Building materials	309	463	13.9	7.4	10.4	34.3	22.0	10.7	1.3	–
Glass	83	605	6.0	1.2	30.1	24.1	20.5	14.5	2.4	1.2
Paper	55	844	1.8	7.3	23.6	21.8	14.6	20.0	10.9	–
Textile	379	884	3.5	7.1	15.1	25.3	13.7	22.4	12.4	0.5
Clothing	458	408	9.6	6.3	20.1	43.0	13.1	5.9	1.8	0.2
Food processing	841	499	6.4	8.2	22.2	32.7	17.7	10.0	2.4	0.4
Printing	122	377	8.2	6.6	24.6	37.7	16.4	5.7	0.8	–

Source: Rocznik Statystyczny.

There is no doubt however, as the data in Table 11.1 show, of the pre-eminence of the public or state sector in the Polish economy. As evident from that data, Polish industry is almost completely in state and co-operative hands. The state's share in employment is smaller than its contribution to GMP and to the stock of fixed capital. This is due to the fact that private industry is concentrated in labour-intensive, quasi-handicraft branches. As a result, average employment in the industrial private sector is very small indeed. This is shown in Table 11.2. Conversely, the average size, by employment, of public sector industrial firms is considerable and employment is concentrated in medium sized and large firms, as shown in Table 11.3. This is a rather typical situation for a centrally-planned economy.

Agriculture plays an exceptional role in the Polish ownership structure, as can be seen directly from Table 11.1. As in the case of industry, the organizational structure, level of employment, and the overall assets structure (measured by the size of the farm) significantly differ between state and co-operative ownership on the one hand, and private on the other. The relevant data are presented in Table 11.4. Until recently any perspective for changes in the agrarian structure had to take into account a legal ceiling on private farms' surface area of 50 ha. But in the political climate since the emergence of the Mazowiecki government possibilities are clearly much more open-ended.

Table 11.4 Characteristics of state and private-owned agriculture (1988)

Type of ownership	Number of units	Average area (ha)
State and co-operatives, total	5,107	1,000
State-owned	2,619	1,630
Co-operatives	2,488	337
Private:		
above 0.5 ha	2,647,000	6
below 0.5 ha	1,205,000	na

Source: As for other tables.

Construction represents the second largest sphere of private activity within the national economy. As with industry, obvious organizational differences exist between private and public sectors. Data on building enterprises and employment are shown in Table 11.5.

Services for households are a traditional area of activity for the private sector. In 1988 the private sector provided 34% of those services. Table 11.6 indicates the range of services rendered by both sectors. In 1989 it became legally possible to provide private services in school education and banking.

Table 11.5 Number of firms and average employment in construction (1988)

Form of ownership	Number of enterprises	Average employment
State-owned and co-operatives, total	1,856	461
state-owned	1,337	600
co-operatives	519	104
Private	128,663	2

Source: As for other tables.

Table 11.6 Services rendered for households (% shares, 1988)

Type of services	Public sector	Private sector
Industrial	36.8	63.2
locksmiths	15.3	84.7
opticians	80.2	19.8
carpenters	15.8	84.2
tailors	23.5	76.5
Constructing	8.7	91.3
Agricultural	96.3	3.7
Transport	84.7	15.3
Commerce	99.8	0.2
Energy	100.0	0.0
Education	99.7	0.3
Culture & art	95.7	4.3
Medical care	42.7	57.3
Finance	100.0	0.0

Source: Rocznik Statystyczny, 1989.

2. Privatization in the government economic programme

The government economic programme, in its stabilization part geared towards fighting inflation, treats the privatization of the state and (pseudo) co-operative enterprises as a starting point for future growth in the entire economy. The ownership pattern aimed at is that of the highly developed European countries. A glance at Table 11.1 shows the scale of the task ahead. For example it is estimated that privatizing 10% of the Polish economy is just about equal to all the privatizations in the world carried out up to this day.

An important social aspect of privatization is the creation of a middle class in Poland that might stabilize recent political changes.

The government economic programme envisages a general framework for the course of privatization which can be summarized as follows:[2]

– shares of privatized enterprises should be generally available to the public;

– the privatization procedures must be transparent, especially the process of selling shares;

– small passive investors and the broadest possible spread of share ownership should be favoured;

– there must be a full transferability of shares on secondary markets.

As can be seen from the above, privatization is not the ultimate goal but a means to build up an effective and flexible market economy with a well functioning capital market.

The programme does not confine 'privatization' to capital investments through share purchases of large enterprises. Other possibilities include so-called small privatizations, the setting up of workshops, and bolstering the growth of the private sector 'from the bottom up' through the birth of new private firms, as well as through nurturing the growth of already existing enterprise. However, one should also note the short-run contradiction between the stabilization programme which reduces real savings and imposes positive real interest rates, and the mobilization of capital needed for privatization.

3. The programme for privatizing the Polish economy

3.1. Ownership changes so far

In the late 1980s opportunities arose for state enterprises to set up companies with the participation of private (domestic and foreign) capital. This often led to a substantial undervaluing of the fixed assets which were transferred to the new company from the state enterprise as its contribution in-kind to equity. Naturally this also produced extra gains for the private partner. This phenomenon, apart from obvious adverse social effects, highlighted one of the basic problems of privatization – how to value the entire firm and its assets in the absence of a genuine owner as a party in the transaction, and of a capital market which could verify prices.

A number of privatizations (with a negligible economic impact) were carried out based upon notions of employee share ownership, where the employees buy a part of the equity capital of the enterprise and lease part of its assets. This sort of privatization is, however, inefficient since it by-passes any capital market and so does not comply with the rules now adopted by the government economic programme.

3.2. Government privatization programme

The government privatization programme is focused mostly on state-owned enterprises that are to be privatized through the public sale of shares. A privatization process, for state firms, was finally sanctioned by Parliament in July 1990.[3] The programme concentrates on state firms because of:
– their dominant role in the economy;
– the far-reaching organizational concentration in comparison with comparable market economies and hence the relatively small number of enterprises to deal with;
– the possibility of identifying the State Treasury as the owner.

The general procedure for privatization of state-owned enterprises is made up of four basic stages.

Stage 1 Identification and evaluation of enterprises selected for privatization
Given the many thousands of state firms (5,823 in industry, 5,107 in agriculture and 1,856 in construction) it is indispensable to make a selection of the best ones, which are to be privatized first. This task is of critical significance to the future of privatization, since it creates certain patterns, and at the same time can build (or destroy) confidence in this completely new form of investing household savings. This is why the first privatized enterprises must ensure high dividends as well as high capital gains. The selection can hardly be based on the previous financial records of the firm since these were shaped under different financial, fiscal and monetary regimes. This means that criteria linked to a 'development potential', such as brand name, competitiveness on international markets, managerial staff performance and technical equipment, are of primary importance.[4]

In the first stage of privatization, a preliminary valuation of the firm must be made. Because of the pricing system which is totally detached from international markets, as well as due to economically suboptimal assets structure, the valuation based on the book value and replacement costs seems to be almost useless. The capitalization of expected earnings, confronted with alternative possibilities of investing savings (the opportunity cost of capital) must be of primary significance.

Stage 2 Enterprise 'commercialization'
Enterprise 'commercialization' mostly means the transformation of a state-owned enterprise into a public limited company. This has two goals:
– to transform the firm into a form that is suitable for capital investments, that is to transform enterprise 'funds' into equity capital;
– an unambiguous definition of property rights with regard to the privatized firm.

The first issue is technical in character but the second touches on an extremely sensitive political problem. The government privatization programme, as well as the law on privatization, both imply that the capital of a joint stock company, resulting from the transformation of a state firm, belongs entirely to the State Treasury. In opposition to that the first privatizations mentioned above, aimed at enlarging employee share ownership, were derived from the idea that part of the capital of the state-owned enterprise belongs to the employees. This view finds expectedly strong support from the employee self-management movement.

Stage 3 Restructuring
In most cases commercialization in the legal sense will not mean commercialization in the economic sense, that is, the emergence of companies able to compete, to stand on their own feet, in the marketplace. Privatization experience, for example in the UK, shows that enterprises frequently need a long and costly restructuring before they can be sold through public subscription. In the Polish situation – characterized by a large number of enterprises to be privatized as well as by strong political pressure to speed up the process – company restructuring cannot go as far or take as long. However, financial restructuring is envisaged and will consist of:
– a 'straightening' of financial statements of the privatized company, according to Western standards;
– treating the expenditures on equipment and other resources which are permanently unproductive as sunk costs;
– in justified cases, granting the firm debt retirement through the State Treasury.

Organizational restructuring is possible and will mostly consist of breaking up monopolistic market structures wherever it is possible. It is also anticipated that the privatized firms will often divest themselves of production and service units which can operate as independent entities. Until recently, in the economy of permanent shortage, it was common for enterprises (for reasons of security of material supply and services) to become excessively vertically integrated and to accumulate service shops, kindergartens and even holiday homes and housing. Today, these may be non-profitable assets. Buyers of shares must be able to view the firm as an attractive and profitable investment. Technical (capital) restructuring is not foreseen in preparing a firm for sale since it is too costly and time-consuming. It is assumed that this restructuring will take place later when the firm is already privatized, especially when the inflow of foreign capital is involved.

Stage 4 Floating
The previous stages are preparation for genuine privatization when the Treasury sells the shares of a joint stock company. With regard to selling, two aspects have special significance: the potential buyers, to whom the offer is addressed; and the manner of the sale.

The potential buyers can be placed in four groups:
– all Polish citizens;
– employees of privatized enterprises;

– local institutional investors;
– foreign investors.

The privatization programme, as described above, implies that the Polish citizen is seen as the main potential buyer of shares, irrespective of the place of employment. The strong social and political message of 'popular share ownership' has serious economic consequences: most of all, shares could be too widely dispersed in comparison with Western economies. In order to offset this weakness institutional investors are to be encouraged. However, there is a basic problem here: a dearth of private financial institutions (we have only two small private insurance companies). The emerging private banks may help overcome this problem but there is also a strong argument for the privatization of some state banks and savings institutions. The creation of mutual funds investing in privatized enterprises is also worth considering.

The employees of the privatized enterprises will be a favoured group of buyers. Preferences will consist in a substantial discount in the sales price of up to 20% of the whole issue. However, these preferences will be awarded to individuals and not to employees treated as a group. The overall value of preferences must be no greater than one year's salary bill. On the other hand, no restrictions with regard to reselling shares on secondary market are envisaged.

Encouraging foreign investors is one of the key tasks of privatization and such investments will enjoy the same fiscal and currency fringe benefits as those of joint-ventures. It is also envisaged that profits from the reinvestment of earnings in Polish currency will be able to be repatriated. Following the example of other countries, in individual privatization cases a ceiling will be placed on foreign investments. That ceiling was set by Parliament on 13 July 1990 at 10% of any share issue, though with special permission it can be extended.

Shares will be sold in different ways but the general rule will be for full disclosure, transparency and competitiveness. For these reasons, public subscription and share auctions will be preferred. This does not exclude private placement in cases justified by trade considerations. Each privatization will take place with maximum publicity and preparation of a full prospectus. On the one hand this should protect the interests of the investor, and on the other it should discredit any charges that state assets are being given away, especially to foreign investors. Well-established foreign firms will take part in the preparation of the prospectus, mainly in the first pilot privatizations.

3.3. Determinants and limits to privatization

The privatization of the Polish economy, from the point of view of its massive scale, as well as its post-central-planning environment, will face several barriers of a diverse nature. At this point two are worth mentioning: the lack of a capital market, and the shortage of household savings.

The relationship between privatization and the lack of a capital market is a good example of a vicious circle. Well-known examples of privatization around the world took place within capital markets which provided comparisons in terms of enterprise valuation and created at the same time channels for the primary sale of shares. In Poland, because no such market exists, the sale of shares will take place – at least at the outset – almost completely in the dark. This will also create the possibility of considerable errors in estimating issue prices. In the years to come, with the emergence of a secondary market, privatization – due to a massive supply of new shares – may lead to serious disturbances in the capital market. Moreover, the lack of a capital market also means the absence of key players on the scene, such as investment banks and institutional investors. The creation of the latter is especially important since they should provide – as was mentioned earlier – an essential source of capital. In this respect, privatization helps to create a well regulated and organized capital market. This market will be controlled, from the fourth quarter of 1990, by a Securities Commission (following the example of the American Stock Exchange Commission – SEC) and will include licensed brokers as well as a stock exchange (starting from the beginning of 1991).

Limitations on the demand side create one of the most serious and controversial problems of mass privatization. Demand determines to a large degree the scale of privatization as well as its temporal sequence. The scale of the problem is marked by extreme views. From one side, the book value of state-owned enterprises, when compared with the savings of the population, leads to the conclusion that the privatization of existing assets would take over a hundred years. From the other side, the radical by-passing of the demand barrier through free distribution of shares, or through symbolic pricing, is proposed.

The adopted privatization programme distances itself from these extremes. It assumes that the prices of shares should emerge from the market place. In this setting, the privatization schedule would determine the supply, whereas the attractiveness of yields from shares in the investor's portfolio would determine demand. It is of the utmost importance to build a market approach into the process from the very beginning, so to create an atmosphere where it is the economic behaviour of investors that matters. Moreover, it is hoped that a more efficient economy, achieved through privatization, will lead to an increase in the private capital stock and will open new possibilities for the further development of the capital market.

Notes

1. M. Bednarski, R. Kokoszczyński and J. Stopyra, 'Kształtowanie się drugiego obiegu gospodarczego w Polsce w latach 1977–1986' (The evolution of the shadow economy in Poland in 1977–1986), *Bank i Kredyt*, 1989, Nos. 8–9, pp. 11–18.
2. The discussion in this chapter is drawn from: Bill on the Privatization of State-Owned Enterprises (draft), mimeo., 1990; *Programme for Ownership Changes in State-Owned Enterprises*, Office of Government Plenipotentiary for Ownership Changes, mimeo., Warsaw, 1990; G. T. Jędrzejczak, 'The Polish Capital Market –

General Concepts', Office of Government Plenipotentiary for Ownership Changes, mimeo., Warsaw, 1990.
3. Parliament accepted the privatization provisions on 13 July 1990. The discussion that follows is based on that Act – Eds.
4. In September 1990 Waldemar Kuczyński was appointed Poland's first minister of privatization and the first firms to be privatized were also identified as: the Silesian cable factory at Czechowice-Dziedzice; the W.W. Norblin steel-rolling mill in Warsaw; the Fampa paperworks at Jelenia Góra; the Inowrocław meat works; the Swarzędz furniture producer; the Krosno glass works; the 'Tonsil' radio plant of Wrzesnia; the Lódz based 'Prochnik' textile firm and the Exbud construction company based at Kielce. The first firms for privatization, profitable companies with a high proportion of exports to the West, have been carefully selected to guarantee domestic and foreign interest.

CHAPTER 12

External disequilibrium and adjustment processes

Krzysztof Kalicki

1. The payments crisis

Errors in economic policy in the 1970s combined with unfavourable changes in the external environment produced the balance of payments crisis that in March 1981 resulted in part suspension of Polish debt service obligations. The long-term effects of excessive indebtedness on national income distribution, on the pace of investment, on consumption and imports were intensified by the political, social and economic chaos of 1981, which further deepened the slump in production.

Towards the end of the 1970s Polish creditors became aware of the growing debt service burden and the coming liquidity crisis. In 1980 the West realized that multilateral rescheduling of Polish debts was inevitable (*Euromoney*, III, 1980). In 1981 creditor governments declared their readiness to reschedule payments and the first steps towards this, at the initiative of France, were taken. The EEC countries confirmed their willingness to reschedule debts but at the same time they reduced the inflow of new loans. Western banks waited for a government lead. They were not willing to increase access to new credits until the political situation had stabilized and the Polish government presented a new and credible economic programme. In these circumstances capitalization of interest was inevitable. Creditors made further finance and economic aid conditional on political changes in Poland. Behind their readiness to talk was an anxiety that Poland would unilaterally declare a debt moratorium.[1] Poland's entry to the IMF (planned initially for November 1981) was intended to ease the debt problem. It was expected at that time that the application would be approved in, at most, nine months.

Despite Poland's poor credit standing, $8.8 bn of loans were obtained in 1980 and $4.9 bn in 1981. Socialist countries' aid was estimated at approximately $2 bn. Under such circumstances it was expected that if Poland continued to foster adjustment processes and to pursue an export-oriented policy the current account might be balanced by 1986.[2] Maintaining production at full capacity and an adequate inflow of new working capital from creditors were necessary conditions to meet this target.

Table 12.1 Imports on credit terms 1981–8 (% of total imports)

Year	1981	1982	1983	1984	1985	1986	1987	1988	1989
$ imports*	73	29	11	4	5	5	5	3	3
Rouble imports	9	18	7	6	8	13	7	1	1

* without revolving credits.
Sources: 'Balance of Payments of Poland for 1987', *Bank i Kredyt*, 1988, No. 7, pp. 29–32; Narodowy Bank Polski, *1987 Biuletyn Informacyjny*, NBP, Warsaw, 1988, pp. 26–8.

The declaration of martial law significantly changed the political, social and economic situation. In response the West imposed economic sanctions. The USA suspended Poland's MFN status. Talks with the Paris Club were broken off. Banks could no longer count on government guarantees for credits granted to Poland which in turn led to a dramatic fall in hard currency imports and dislocation of production dependent on supplies from the West. This was compensated for only to a limited extent by increases in loan financing from the COMECON countries (mainly the USSR – see Table 12.1).

In the case of outright debt repudiation or a unilateral declaration of moratorium the following retaliatory measures were envisaged: freezing of all Polish bank deposits, attachment of Polish assets abroad, filing civil suits with creditors' countries' courts and demanding from creditors' governments enforcement of 'protection' clauses.[3] However, such a development would also have damaged the banks. A stalemate ensued. In spite of martial law Western governments did not declare Poland insolvent but the inflow of new medium- and long-term loans dropped dramatically to a level that was negligible from the viewpoint of the needs of the economy. In this situation, loan financing from the COMECON countries increased considerably despite the fact that many of them were also facing economic difficulties (see Table 12.2).

Financing problems meant that imports from Western countries had to be cut. As a consequence, capacity utilization in Polish manufacturing industry fell sharply from 83.4% in 1977 to 64.2% in 1982. A significant proportion of capacity continued to remain idle in the years ahead.

Table 12.2 Inflow of new loans 1980–9

	1980	1981	1982	1983	1984	1985	1986	1987	1988	1989
$ bn	8.7	4.9	1.5	0.6	0.2	0.3	0.3	0.3	0.3	0.3
Roubles bn	0.2	0.7	1.4	0.6	0.7	0.8	1.6	0.8	0.2	0.1

Source: As for Table 12.1.

2. Economic policy targets

After the imposition of martial law the government had to redevelop economic policy. Its main objectives became:
- Minimizing the effects of economic sanctions;
- Substituting Comecon supplies for the shortfall in hard currency imports;
- Expanding hard currency exports with an attempt to re-establish normal financial relations through the generation of a trade surplus which would enable further debt servicing;
- Protecting the level of consumption of low income groups;
- Slowing investment and axeing the most capital-intensive projects in favour of those increasing the export potential of the economy;
- Restoring market equilibrium and reducing inflationary pressure.

These targets were to be achieved through market-oriented systemic reforms. In addition, no more than 25% of export earnings was to be devoted to debt service. A trade surplus was to be generated by curtailing hard currency imports and expanding exports. Cuts in hard currency imports were supposed to be compensated for by a rise in imports from the socialist countries. Hard currency export expansion was, in turn, to be rooted in a comprehensive export-promotion policy using such instruments as the exchange rate, export earnings retention accounts,[4] tax relief and bonuses for exporters granted by the Minister of Foreign Trade.

3. Adjustment processes in foreign trade

The foreign trade situation was influenced not only by developments in the domestic economy but also by the external environment. Due to limited access to Western loans the share of imports of goods and services in GMP (Gross Material Product) declined from 17% in 1980 to 7% in 1983 (balance of payments data). Imports from the socialist countries also fell but by a much smaller amount (Figures 12.1 and 12.2).

The drastic reduction in imports led to a breakdown in exports of goods and services and to a decline in their share in GMP from 27% in 1980 to 17% in 1983. From 1983 the share of exports and imports in GMP gradually rose although the 1980 level had not been achieved by 1988. The current account balance deteriorated with both the convertible and the Rouble area. Poland had quickly to undertake adjustment measures to bring about an improvement in the hard currency current account, partly at the expense of the balance on the Rouble account (1982–5). However the Rouble balance improved substantially from 1987 (see Figure 12.3). Notwithstanding many difficulties, in the 1980s Poland took steps to improve the current account balance with both the industrialized and the socialist countries. The results may seem unsatisfactory, but the hard currency current account has been weighed down by interest due on earlier loans, amounting to about $3 bn per year ($29.4 bn altogether over

EXTERNAL DISEQUILIBRIUM 121

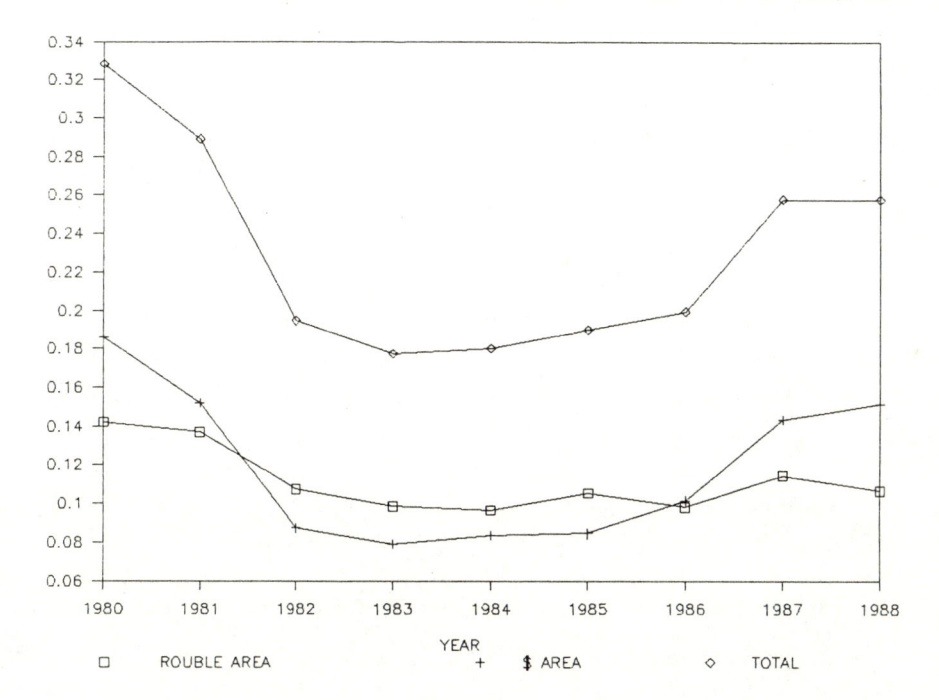

Figure 12.1 Import/Net Material Product 1980–8

1981–9). The noticeable early 1980s shift in trade balance trends testifies to Polish efforts to overcome financial difficulties – the hard currency trade balance improved considerably, and in 1988 a surplus was recorded in both trading areas (see Figure 12.4). However this 'success' was short-lived and in 1989 the hard currency trade surplus was reduced to only $742 mn (balance of payments data).

The earlier improvement in the convertible trade balance (the cumulative surplus during 1980–9 amounted to $5.7 bn) was achieved partly thanks to the possibility of sustaining a deficit in the trade balance *vis-à-vis* the Rouble area. The biggest deficit occurred in 1980–1. After a certain improvement in 1982, the deficit continued to grow in the following years until 1985, after which it began to decline. The cumulative trade deficit with socialist countries totalled R6.1 bn in 1980–9. Planned targets however were not fully met and this was due, among other things, to difficulties in financing trade – despite strenuous efforts Poland failed to secure any significant financial co-operation from the West. Poland had to pay cash for imports and very often advance payments were required (about 70% of imports required down payments).

The attempt speedily to generate a surplus in the trade balance led to a decline in consumption and investment and a slow down of economic growth which

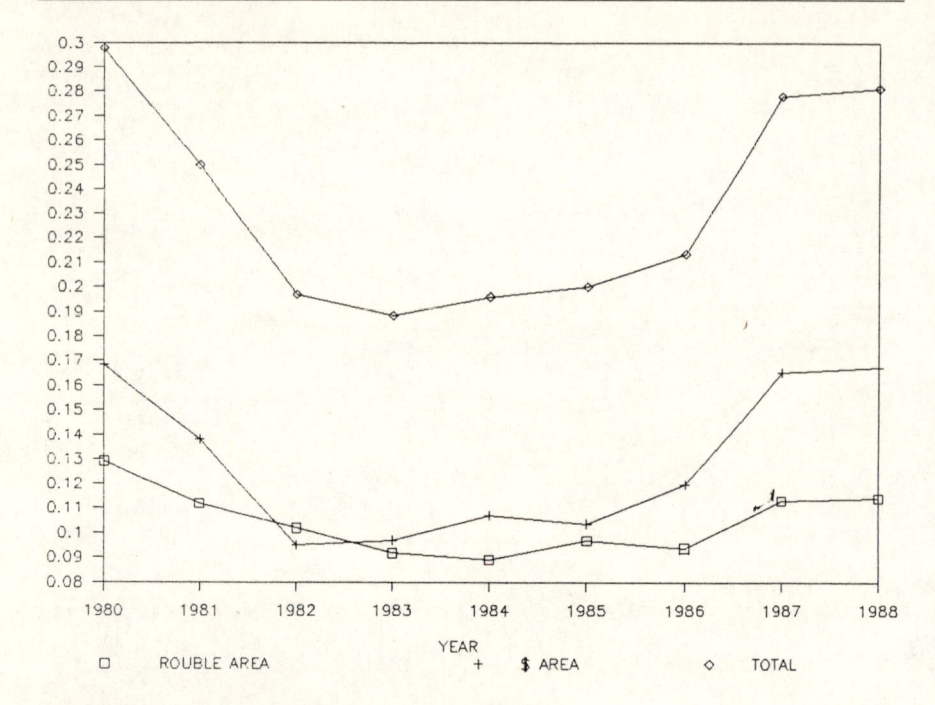

Figure 12.2 Export/Net Material Product 1980–8

gradually diminished Poland's long-run ability fundamentally to improve the trade balance.

Placing the entire cost of overcoming the debt crisis on Poland seems to be impossible since the Polish economy requires increased capital outlays for modernization as well as imported supplies.

In 1980–9 trade in services with the convertible currency area was almost balanced (the deficit was $171 mn), whereas a considerable surplus was obtained with the Rouble area (R 1.2 bn). Fast growth of exports of construction and transport services (sea and rail) was the main factor behind the upward trend in export earnings. Tourism and foreign travel have been the main debit items on the services account. Foreign exchange transfers were a major item easing the pressure on the hard currency balance of payments, mainly thanks to favourable interest rates on the convertible currency deposits of the population (33% of all net transfers) and private purchases in the hard currency (Pewex) stores (57.6% of all net transfers). The balance of transfers was consistently positive over the 1970s and 1980s (except only for 1982) and has grown steadily over the whole period. Over recent years the value of those transfers has exceeded $1.4 bn annually ($8.2 bn over 1980–9). It needs to be emphasised that net receipts under this heading were equivalent in 1988 to over 156% of the trade surplus

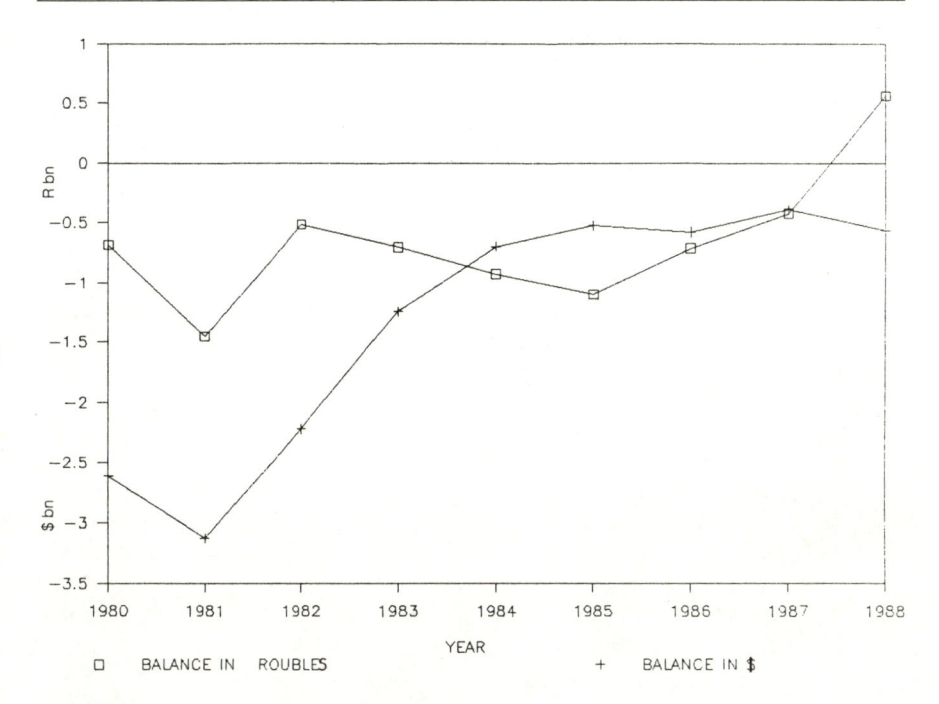

Figure 12.3 Current account balance 1980–8

(477% in 1989) and became the most important source in debt service finance. The balance of Rouble transfers was of minor importance and was only slightly in surplus over the period considered (for example TR 5 mn in 1989).

Foreign trade adjustments were accompanied by parallel changes in domestic absorption aimed at reducing aggregate demand. The efficiency of these processes depended on the speed of shifts in the distribution of national income, the rate of growth of consumption and investment, the intensity of inflation and the proper tuning of these aggregates with the demand and supply of money on the domestic market (Table 12.3).

It was only from 1982 that the growth rate of NMP produced exceeded the growth of NMP distributed but this trend prevailed throughout the 1980s. In the 1980s capital expenditure bore the brunt of the adjustment process.

The fall in consumption was much smaller in comparison with the decline in investment: investment cutbacks in turn mostly affected sectors of material production. It was an important weakness of the adjustment processes that the deepest cuts affected capital outlays on machinery and equipment. Another shortcoming was the much sharper restriction of personal consumption as compared to collective consumption. It was only in the later 1980s that this policy shifted. The rate of inflation, although very high for a centrally-planned

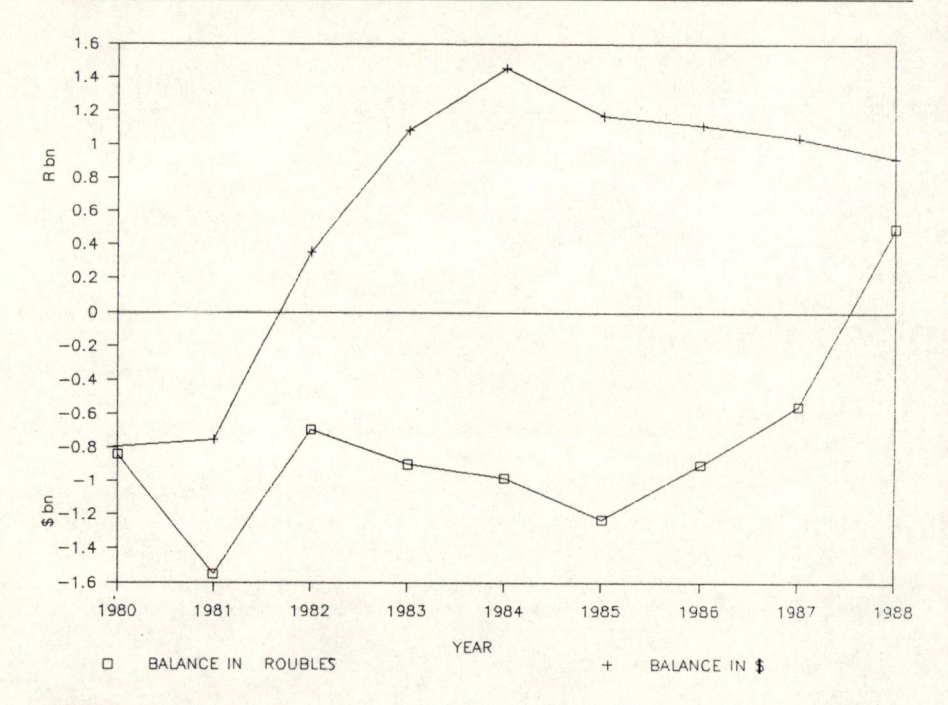

Figure 12.4 Trade balance 1980–8

economy, did not bring about a significant fall in consumption nor a sufficient reduction in excessive monetary resources. The policy of delaying official price increases resulted only in increasing the money supply and this was not matched by an equivalent increase in the supply of goods and services. The scale of monetary disequilibrium, however, tended slowly to diminish until 1987, owing to the depreciation of monetary resources as a result of inflation. Adjustment processes in the balance of payments negatively affected the domestic market exacerbating monetary disequilibrium. This contradiction resulted in a further deepening of internal imbalance and pressures to increase imports and hence indebtedness which in turn has limited, as a feed-back, the effectiveness of measures aimed at improving the balance of payments position.

Poland achieved the above results on the current account in an unfavourable external environment. The expectation of fast growth in economic efficiency through systemic reforms was disappointed. The reforms, implemented incoherently, failed to bring about radical changes in productivity and the import intensity of national income. Every 1% growth in national income requires on average almost twice as much in imports. The results in foreign trade have been achieved at the cost of accelerated inflation, złoty devaluation, growing disequilibrium on official markets and sharp price rises in the shadow

Table 12.3 Variables describing adjustment processes in foreign trade 1980–9

Year	1980	1981	1982	1983	1984	1985	1986	1987	1988	1989
% growth over previous year constant prices										
Total imports	–1.9	–16.9	–13.7	5.2	8.6	7.9	4.9	4.5	9.4	na
Imports from hard currency area	–7.2	–31.5	–24.2	6.6	7.4	13.4	–1.9	10.7	22.5	4.4
Imports from rouble area	2.4	–6.3	–5.6	4.4	9.2	4.6	9.4	0.4	0.0	–5.8
Total exports	–4.2	–19.0	8.7	10.3	9.5	1.3	4.9	4.8	9.1	na
Exports to hard currency area	5.0	–22.1	0.9	12.4	9.0	–6.5	1.4	7.1	14.2	–0.7
Exports to rouble area	–9.5	–17.0	16.6	8.3	10.0	8.1	7.6	2.8	5.7	–0.8
Average interest on debts (%)										
Dollar	10.2	12.9	11.6	11.0	10.2	9.2	8.7	8.2	8.3	8.4
Roubles	1.7	1.8	3.1	3.0	3.3	3.7	3.3	4.0	4.4	8.2
Devaluation złoty/dollar in (%)	5.5	28.2	54.9	13.8	28.3	17.1	33.6	34.2	59.3	1200
Increase in cost of living %	9.1	24.4	101.5	23.1	15.7	14.4	17.3	25.5	59.0	244.0
Import elasticity of national income	0.95	0.71	0.42	1.15	0.64	0.42	0.98	0.46	0.51	4.5
Terms of trade	98.4	99.6	99.1	96.0	98.6	102.5	101.9	103.7	101.1	102.0
Rate of growth of NMP distributed (constant prices) (%)	–6.0	–10.5	–10.5	5.6	5.0	3.8	5.0	1.8	4.7	–0.0
Rate of growth of NMP produced (constant prices) (%)	–6.0	–12.0	–5.5	6.0	5.6	3.4	4.9	1.9	4.9	–0.8
Ratio of NMP produced to NMP distributed	100.0	98.3	105.5	100.4	100.6	99.6	100.1	100.1	100.2	100.0
Rate of growth of (%)										
Consumption	2.1	–4.6	–11.6	5.7	4.4	2.9	4.9	2.9	3.3	na
Investment	–30.2	–28.3	–7.4	5.4	6.4	6.2	4.5	0.1	8.0	na
Money supply	9.6	25.7	38.6	17.4	21.0	22.1	28.9	32.1	61.1	476.0

Source: Own calculations based on *Rocznik Statystyczny*, GUS, Warsaw, various years.

economy. The only favourable factors worth noting in recent years were the slight improvement of terms of trade and the fall in nominal interest rates on outstanding debts, nevertheless real interest rates still remaining high (Table 12.3).

4. External adjustment processes

The beginning of the 1980s was characterized by a significant cumulation of principal and interest on loans falling due (Table 12.4). Simultaneously, the inflow of new loans in convertible currencies sharply dropped during 1982–8. Debt service commitments exceeded debt-service capacity in the years following 1981. The only solution acceptable to both official and unofficial creditors was to renegotiate debt repayment. In 1982 Poland owed $10 bn in guaranteed loans, $6.9 bn in commercial banks' credits, $1.8 bn in credits from socialist countries, $0.4 bn from Arab countries, $0.1 bn from Polish banks' foreign subsidiaries and $2.5 bn from other countries (clearing payment agreements).

First steps towards debt rescheduling were taken in March 1981 at the Paris Club forum and ended on 27 April 1981 with an agreement providing for deferred payment of $1.6 bn of principal and $463 mn of interest due in 1981: this was equal to 90% of the amount actually due. At that time Poland managed to obtain terms no worse than other debtors. The interest rate however was allowed to float and in this period it moved upwards. This agreement assumed that normal credit relations would be resumed and new loans amounting from $3 bn to $3.5 bn would be obtained.[5] Negotiations concerning the rescheduling of payments due in 1982 took place in the autumn of 1981. After the declaration of martial law and the imposition of economic sanctions the talks broke off. Poland stopped all payments to state-supported creditors. Outstanding payments were simply capitalized and the share of guaranteed loans rose to account for two-thirds of the total value of hard currency debt.

Table 12.4 Medium- and long-term hard currency maturity payments 1982–9 (%)

	1982	1983	1984	1985	1986	1987	1988	1989
Total	9.7	7.1	5.5	5.0	6.2	6.3	6.7	6.6
Interest	6.7	4.2	2.8	2.4	3.5	3.3	3.6	3.5
Principal	3.0	2.9	2.7	2.6	2.7	3.0	3.1	3.1
Debt service/exports ratio	1.77	1.16	0.86	0.78	0.90	0.82	0.78	0.81

Source: NBP (National Bank of Poland) materials.

In 1984 debt negotiations were resumed, leading to a second agreement signed on 15 July 1984 which rescheduled 100% of principal and 100% of interest due in 1982–4. The next agreement (19 November 1985) covered overdue amounts in 1985 and shifted payment to the 1990s. Despite a certain

Table 12.5 Official debt rescheduling 1981–90

	1981	1985	1986	1987	1990
Liabilities, $ bn	2.1	11.5	1.4	8.9	9.5
Principal	1.63	7.65	1.1	3.3	na
Interest	0.47	3.83	0.3	5.5	na
% of rescheduled principal	90	100	100	100	100
Loan maturity (years)	8	10	10	10	14
Grace period (years)	4	5	5	5	8
Repayment dates	84–9	90	96	93–7	97–2004

Source: NBP materials; J. Mościcki, 'Po umowie paryskiej' (After the Paris Agreement), *Życie Gospodarcze*, No. 30, 1985.

normalization of credit relations with creditor countries, the expected inflow of new loans did not materialize and in 1986 overdue commitments reappeared. The next agreement was signed on 16 December 1987 with the Paris Club and rescheduled payments due in 1986–8 (see Table 12.5). A further agreement was signed in February 1990 and rescheduled payments due in 1989–91. The main novel feature of this agreement was the extension to fourteen years of loan maturities with eight years' grace.

Martial law did not end talks concerning the rescheduling of principal and interest owed to private banks: agreements were signed as the need arose (see Table 12.6).

Table 12.6 Terms of rescheduling private banks' loans 1981–8

	1981	1982	1983	1984	1986	1988
Planned rescheduling:						
$ bn	2.1	3.5	1.7	1.6	1.6	8.2
Principal	2.1	2.4	1.2	1.6	1.6	na
Interest	0	1.1	0.5	0	0	na
Actually agreed:						
% of principal rescheduled	95	95	95	95	95–80	100
Loan maturity	7.5	7.5	10	10	10	15
Grace period (years)	4	4	5	5	6	0
Repayment period	85–7	86–9	88–92	88–93	90–4	88–2002
Spread over LIBOR	1¾	1¾	1⅞	1¾	1¾	13/16
Percentage of interest rescheduled	0	50	65	0	na	na

Sources: Financial Times, 4 August 1987; and NBP, 1988.

At the beginning of 1981 Poland owed the banks $7.7 bn. During the 1980s all principal payments falling due were rescheduled but interest was, more or less dutifully, paid so the total amount owed to private institutions did not change significantly. It should be noted that debts have been rescheduled under prevailing market conditions with the extra costs passed on to the debtor. Moreover the rescheduling outlook was always short term until the 1986 agreement covering payments due in 1984–7 which was the first one after martial law to look ahead to future repayments allowing a reduction in uncertainty concerning the scale of future debt service.

The agreement signed with the banks in 1988 was more advantageous for Poland because consolidation and rescheduling looked ahead to future repayments due in 1988–93. It also provided for the possibility for interest rate adjustments, conversion of debts into equity in Polish companies and issuing of exit bonds.

In 1987 a debt rescheduling agreement with the USSR was reached postponing payments of principal until 1998–2003.

In conclusion, the balance of payments situation in Poland in 1981–9, despite great effort, improved only slightly. During this period the country repaid $12.3 bn in interest out of a total due of $26.9 bn. The inflow of new loans was negligible and amounted to only $8.5 bn net. Over 1981–8 the total amount of rescheduled and overdue obligations on medium- and long-term loans amounted to about $29 bn, compared to $5.9 bn repaid. Poland did however manage to reduce the level of short-term debt and increase hard currency reserves.

In the case of socialist countries debt service amounted over 1981–8 to R 1.9 bn and was fully repaid. However, owing to growing imports on credit terms, particularly in the first half of the 1980s, total indebtedness increased to R 6.5 bn in 1988 then fell in 1989 to R 5.8 bn. The major part (97%) of debt was due to the USSR and the two CMEA banks. The remaining 3% was owed to other countries, which reflects the modest scale of assistance extended to Poland by the rest of the CMEA.

Table 12.7 Indebtedness 1980–9 (end year)

Year	1980	1981	1982	1983	1984	1985	1986	1987	1988	1989
Roubles bn	1.5	3.1	3.7	3.8	4.8	5.6	6.5	6.6	6.5	5.8
$ bn	24.1	25.9	26.4	26.4	26.8	29.3	33.5	39.2	39.2	41.4
Total $ bn*	25.6	28.4	29.4	29.1	29.6	32.6	36.6	42.1	42.2	42.9
Internal hard currency liabilities $ bn	na	na	na	na	na	2.1	2.7	3.9	5.2	7.2

* R/dollar conversion factors were calculated from the rates applied in Polish foreign trade.
Source: GUS, *Rocznik Statystyczny*, Warsaw, 1989.

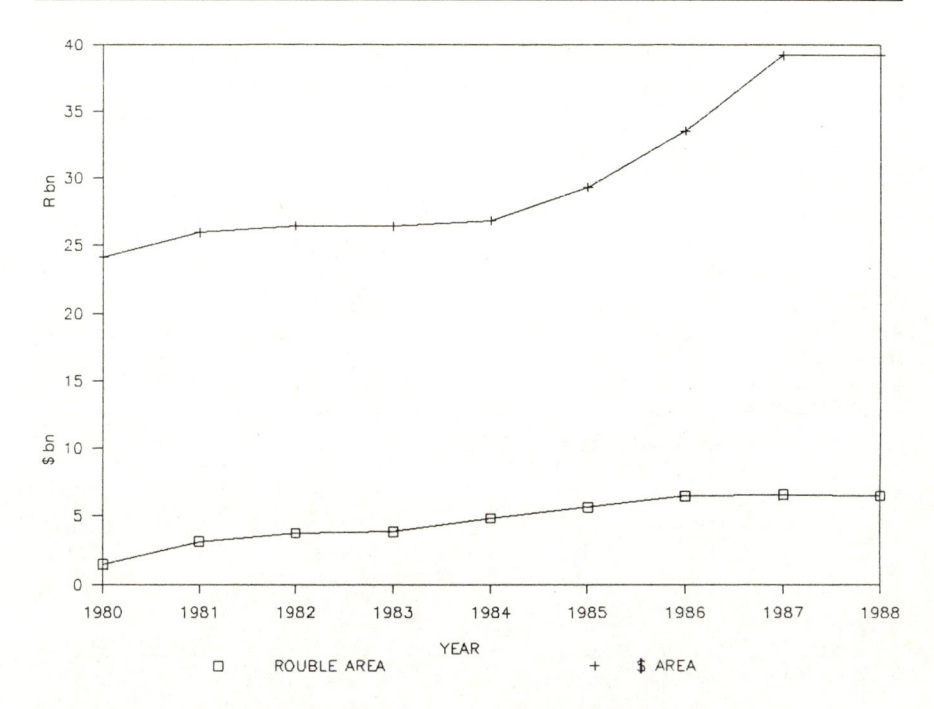

Figure 12.5 Debt in Transferable Roubles and dollars 1980–8

Overall, Polish indebtedness increased in the 1980s, though its rate of growth declined each year (see Table 12.7, Figure 12.5).

The hard currency obligations guaranteed by governments constitutes about 65% of all outstanding payments, and those due to commercial banks 25%. Remaining hard currency indebtedness consists mainly of CMEA loans and supplier's credits. Poland's main hard currency creditors are: West Germany (about 20%), France (about 11%), Austria (9%), USA (about 8%), and the UK (about 7%). Approximately 80% of all Polish debts are owed to OECD countries, and the remaining 20% to developing and the COMECON countries (10% each).

Any account of Poland's hard currency indebtedness is not complete if it fails to mention the obligations of Polish banks towards citizens and enterprises with convertible currencies deposits. These amounted to $2.06 bn in 1985, $2.69 bn in 1986, $3.9 bn in 1987, $5.2 bn in 1988 (including $3.6 bn on personal accounts), and $7.2 bn in 1989.

Table 12.8 Selected variables reflecting Poland's financial situation 1980–9 (%)

	1980	1981	1982	1983	1984	1985	1986	1987	1988	1989
Debt/exports ratio										
Rouble area	22	50	50	46	52	56	58	56	50	45
$ area	271	424	484	437	420	461	489	511	452	511
Interest/exports ratio										
Rouble area	0	1	2	1	2	2	2	2	2	4
$ area	28	55	56	48	43	41	40	39	36	43
Interest paid/interest due										
$ area	na	68	61	55	46	47	42	31	31	31

Source: Own calculations based on data from Table 12.1.

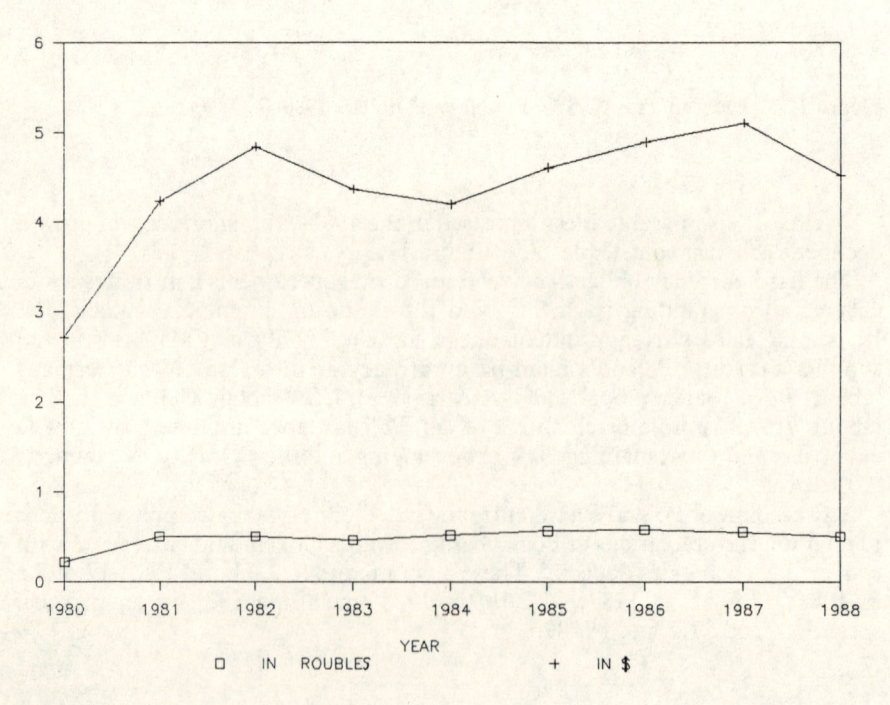

Figure 12.6 Debt/export 1980–8

EXTERNAL DISEQUILIBRIUM 131

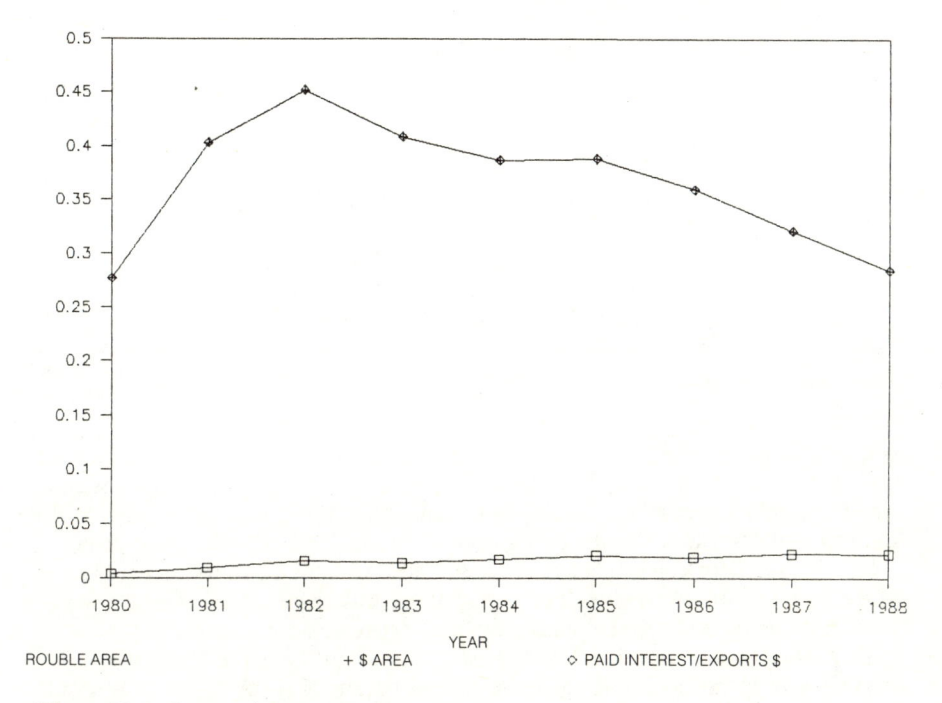

Figure 12.7 Interest/export 1980–8

5. Repayment outlook

Better export performance in 1988 resulted in some improvement in indebtedness indicators (see Table 12.8, Figures 12.6–12.7). But it was short-lived. In 1989 hard currency exports fell in volume by 0.4% and the current account deficit increased to around $1.4 bn.

An additional threat for the future stems from the cumulation of debt service payments in the beginning of the 1990s, and this is the outcome of earlier rescheduling agreements (see Table 12.9).

The outlook for solving the Rouble debt problem looked, until very recently, more promising. The current account deficit with socialist countries was mostly due to the delayed effects of the second oil crisis resulting in higher oil prices;[6] as oil prices fell terms of trade with the Rouble area improved and a current account surplus was easier to achieve. In 1988, for the first time, Poland's Rouble indebtedness fell slightly. However the events of 1989–90, and in particular the imminent move from the 'Transferable Rouble' to the dollar in settling international transactions, have considerably confused the 'soft currency' trade and debt picture. Clearly, the Soviet demand that Poland must pay in hard currency for commodities supplied is immediately disadvantageous for Poland

Table 12.9 Expected debt service 1989–98 ($ bn)

	1989	1990	1991	1992	1993	1994	1995	1996	1997	1998
Paris Club	1.122	2.469	2.676	2.629	4.297	4.288	4.281	1.742	1.721	0.029
Non-guaranteed credits	0.121	0.124	1.081	0.149	0.149	0.408	0.408	0.816	0.816	0.816
Other	0.322	0.302	0.327	0.418	0.308	0.310	0.348	0.385	0.375	0.461
Total	1.565	2.895	4.084	3.196	4.754	5.006	5.037	2.943	2.912	1.306

Source: National Bank of Poland, Warsaw, 1988.

and places a greater short-term strain on the balance of payments. Poland, on the other hand, was locked, in 1990, in negotiations with the USSR over an 'appropriate' revaluation of Rouble debt to take account, amongst others, of the hitherto under-valued Polish contributions to COMECON investment projects.

The Polish debt crisis is still very acute and has slowed investment, created idle capacities due to the insufficient supply of raw materials, slowed economic growth, widened the technological gap, and depressed consumption.

In 1986 some economists warned that the continuation of the early 1980s strategy would not improve the economic situation. On the contrary it would lead in particular to a growing fuels and energy deficit. By the 1990s the trade surplus would fall and the balance of payments deteriorate. A second scenario assumed debt repayment through a drastic decrease in internal absorption but this would have meant returning to administrative methods of management. There may have been a short-run improvement in the balance of payments but it would have been accompanied by a fall in investment and would have further reduced future repayment possibilities. The third scenario, advocated by the majority of economists, argued for radical market-oriented economic reforms which would give room for individual initiatives, improve organization, raise economic efficiency, encourage savings, stimulate material-saving technologies and restructure the economy. This scenario would require in the first stage stabilization of the trade surplus with both trading areas, in order to accelerate debt repayments in the mid-1990s, thanks to faster economic growth.[7] The events of 1989 pushed Poland towards the third scenario, that is radical, market-oriented economic reforms.

The establishment of the Mazowiecki government and the radical programme of market-oriented reforms devised by the Finance Minister, Leszek Balcerowicz, brought a major change in the attitude of creditor countries towards Poland in 1989–90. Government policy began to follow IMF recommendations and formal IMF backing was won in 1990. The main target of the government is, in the first stage, to overcome inflation through monetary and credit policy. But many other changes are in the pipeline.

The IMF agreement opens the way to stand-by credits, worth $700 mn, as well as loans from the World Bank, including a structural adjustment loan (SAL). Some privatization measures will be supported by the International Finance Corporation. Poland is looking to the Paris Club to reschedule repayments and relieve the debt burden as well as to reduce the amount of the outstanding debt owed to commercial banks to its current market value (the Brady Plan). The government plans to tighten co-operation with the EEC in order to liberalize trade relations and capital transfer.

The second stage of the reforms provides for a far-reaching privatization of the economy, establishment of a free market for commodities, labour, capital, money and foreign exchange with corresponding changes in financial, tax (universal income tax, value added tax), foreign exchange and budgetary laws. The latest news concerning financial aid for Poland, estimated at approximately $10 bn (equal, incidentally, to the amount initially 'requested' in the summer of 1989 by Professor Witold Trzeciakowski) creates a chance to speed up economic growth and for reform to succeed. The aid in question would be granted partly in the form of debt rescheduling, and partly in terms of the inflow of new venture capital. The direct support promised by the West in early 1990 amounted to:

USA $177 mn (foodstuffs)
EEC $120 mn (foodstuffs)
France $90 mn (new credits)
Sweden $45 mn (environment protection)
UK $40 mn (training of managers)

Support which was under consideration in late 1989 included:

IMF $2,500 mn (new credits)
USA $2,000 mn (relief in debt repayment)
USA $2,000 mn (development aid)
West Germany $1,300 mn (new loans, credit guarantees)
West Germany $500 mn (debt repayment in złoties)
World Bank $300 mn (aid for agriculture)
European Investment Bank ECU 1,000 mn (jointly for Poland and Hungary for 3 years.

It is impossible to know how many of these promises will be fulfilled. In the new political situation, however, creditors appear willing to make terms easier. The liberalization of regulations concerning foreign direct investment in Poland creates an opportunity to improve the technical level and organization of industry, banking services and exports. Debt-equity swaps have a role here too. Perhaps a variant of the Brady Plan might be applied consisting of: buying out debt at a discount; debt-to-treasury bonds swaps; debt-to-equity swaps; or debt-to-environmental protection swaps.

In the last quarter of 1989 and at the beginning of 1990 many crucial changes in economic policy took place, including:
- the abolishing of price control and central planning, with introduction of more elements of a market economy, better conditions for foreign investors, regulations allowing the creation of a capital market,
- implementation of internal convertibility of the złoty accompanied by its sharp devaluation, introduction of a uniform customs tariff,
- substantial reduction of the budget deficit, tightening of money and credit control, 'hardening' of the budget constraint,
- beginning of the de-monopolization and privatization process, coupled with an encouragement to domestic and external competition,
- reform of the banking system, a comprehensive reform of the budget and tax system.

Results in the first quarter of 1990 do not allow any unambiguous assessment to be made. On the one hand the rate of inflation was brought down but at the same time real output fell by nearly 30% compared to the first quarter of 1989. The slump in output exceeded by far the target set out in the adjustment plan (–5.0%). Unemployment, though not in proportion to the fall in output, also emerged. At the same time exports to Western countries increased by 8.5% and imports decreased by 19.5% with a first quarter trade surplus of $777.9 mn. Exports to the CMEA countries rose by 0.7% and imports fell by 28.5% yielding a trade surplus of R 970.8 mn.

Even if, optimistically, economic growth does pick up in the near future, Poland's indebtedness is bound to grow in the coming years and balancing the current account will only be possible in the second half of the 1990s.

Notes

1. See R. Portes, *The Polish Crisis: Western Economic Policy Options*, The Royal Institute of International Affairs, London, February 1981.
2. See J. Tomorowicz, 'Jak nalać z pustego' (How to pour from the empty), *Polityka*, No. 49, 1986.
3. See L. Sandler, 'Banks study possible reply to repudiation', *The Wall Street Journal*, 10 July 1984.
4. See Chapter 3 by Dariusz Rosati.
5. See J. Mościcki, 'Po umowie paryskiej' (After the Paris agreement), *Życie Gospodarcze*, No. 30, 1985.
6. See Konsultacyjna Rada Gospodarcza, 'Handel Zagraniczny' (Foreign trade), *Życie Gospodarcze*, No. 17, 1984.
7. See *Raport o sytuacji i perspektywach gospodarczych Polski w latach 1987–1996* (Report on the economic situation in Poland and prospects for 1987–1996), ed. J. Pawilno-Pacewicz et al., Warsaw, 1987.

♦ CHAPTER 13 ♦

Foreign trade

Ryszard Rapacki

1. General picture

Over the last several decades foreign trade has performed a marginal role in the Polish economy, both in quantitative and in qualitative terms. Until 1978, the last pre-crisis year, Poland's share in world trade remained more or less constant at around 1%. Compared to the country's physical and economic potential this was clearly a disappointing and inadequate performance (see Table 13.1). In the 1980s Poland's participation in both world and European trade deteriorated sharply (by more than 50%) leaving the country even more at the margin of international merchandise flows. The share of Polish exports and imports in

Table 13.1 Poland in a world and European context 1978–88 (%)

	share in Europe				share in the world			
	1978	1980	1985	1988	1978	1980	1985	1988
Area	3.0	3.0	3.0	3.0	0.2	0.2	0.2	0.2
Population	5.2	5.2	5.3	5.4	0.8	0.8	0.8	0.8
Production of mineral fuels	6.8	5.5	5.0	5.0	2.3	1.9	1.9	1.8
Production of electricity	3.6	3.5	3.4	3.4	1.5	1.5	1.4	1.4
Imports (current prices)	2.2	1.4	1.2	1.1	1.2	0.9	0.5	0.4
Exports (current prices)	2.0	2.1	1.3	1.1	1.1	0.8	0.6	0.5

Sources: Yearbook of International Statistics 1984, Retrospective Review, GUS, Warsaw, 1985; GUS *Rocznik Statystyczny* 1980, 1989.

total world trade over 1978–88 was not only much below the standards of industrialized, traditionally outward-oriented economies, but also lower than that of other COMECON countries as well as some developing countries at a similar level of development (for example, Spain, Mexico, Brazil, South Korea). This disproportion increased significantly over the 1980s especially with regard to the newly industrialized countries.

The openness of an economy can also be measured in terms of per capita trade flows. Poland's position in this respect was the lowest among European and middle-income developing countries. Exports per capita totalled $369 in 1988 ($508 in 1980) with imports at $323. The value of average trade turnover per inhabitant was almost eight times lower than the average for the EEC countries and almost three times lower than the average for the European COMECON countries.

One more widely used indicator of the openness of an economy is the share of exports in national income. Taking due account of existing deficiencies in methodologies of international comparisons, especially involving countries with non-convertible currencies, the data available again clearly indicate the poor performance of Polish foreign trade and its negligible role in the country's economic development. In 1987 the ratio of exports to GMP (Gross Material Product) amounted in Poland to 19.0% (21.3% in 1978), which compares unfavourably with such countries as Belgium and Luxembourg (75%), the Netherlands (67%), Denmark (38%), West Germany (37%), UK (30%), Bulgaria (48%), Czechoslovakia (43%) and South Korea (38%).

In qualitative terms, foreign trade has always been viewed as a residual by successive Polish governments. Its role was simply to supply the economy with commodities not available locally or in short local supply. Comparative advantage considerations were either absent or of secondary importance. As a consequence, the main function of exports was to earn foreign exchange to finance imports. The exports themselves tended chiefly to be items in 'abundant' supply. Their profitability (or lack of it) was of little interest. Autarchy and lack of specialization meant that the range of sectors providing export commodities was quite broad. Principal exports, particularly to industrialized countries, included unprocessed and semi-processed commodities, such as minerals (coal, sulphur, zinc, copper), agricultural raw materials and foodstuffs, simpler industrial goods (components, parts, metal products, textiles), chemicals and miscellaneous manufactures.

Until the early 1980s the state held a monopoly over foreign trade operations. In practice, except for marginal deals, all export–import transactions were carried out exclusively by several narrowly specialized foreign trade organizations (FTOs) acting as intermediaries between foreign markets and domestic producers/users of traded goods. The latter were entirely cut off from international markets since the final prices they received (were charged) as suppliers or recipients had nothing to do whatsoever with actual prices paid/charged by foreign counterparts. This isolation was additionally strengthened by the non-convertibility of the currency, multiple, artificial exchange rates and a sophisticated 'equalization system' aimed at levelling the financial situation of profitable and non-profitable export producers and import users.

2. From the 1970s to the present

The 1970s witnessed a very fast trade expansion in Poland, especially as far as imports from industrialized countries were concerned. In 1971–6 overall imports in constant prices grew by 125.2% and those from Western countries by 263%. Fast growth of imports from this area was not matched by a corresponding increase in exports which rose by only 68%.

The resulting deficit was covered with an increasing flow of foreign loans. But growing difficulties in servicing a growing external debt led eventually (from 1977) to sharp cuts in imports from industrialized countries. This produced several problems and contributed substantially to the 1979–82 economic crisis in Poland.

The slump suffered in exports was shorter and less severe than the crisis in the whole economy. An absolute decrease in GMP was first recorded in 1979 and lasted for four years. Exports, on the other hand, fell in real terms only in 1980 and 1981, and in 1982 were just 10% lower than in 1978 (see Table 13.2). Imports, particularly from Western countries, did much worse (see Tables 13.2 and 13.3).

The average rates of growth for total imports hid two diverging trends. Imports from centrally-planned economies (equivalent more or less to the so-called 'trading area I' or non-convertible area) fell only over the 1981–2 period and only by 11.5%. The decline in imports from non-socialist countries (the so-called 'trading area II' or convertible area), was much more dramatic and was

Table 13.2 Growth of GMP, exports and imports 1980–8

	1980	1982	1985	1986	1987	1988	1989
GMP produced							
% growth rate	–4.3	–4.8	3.3	4.8	2.1	4.7	0
1978 = 100	94.7	80.1	92.6	97.0	98.7	103.2	103.2
Exports							
% growth rate	–4.2	8.7	1.3	4.9	4.8	9.4	–0.7
1978 = 100	102.3	90.1	110.2	115.6	121.1	132.5	131.6
Imports							
% growth rate	–1.9	–13.7	7.9	4.9	4.5	8.7	–0.7
1978 = 100	96.9	69.5	85.7	89.9	93.9	102.1	101.4

Source: based on *Rocznik Statystyczny*, GUS, Warsaw, 1986, 1987, 1988 and 1989 *Rzeczpospolita* 1 February 1990.

Table 13.3 Growth of exports and imports with different trading areas 1980–8 (constant prices)

	1980	1982	1985	1986	1987	1988
Rouble exports						
% growth rate	91.0	113.5	107.0	108.7	104.8	108.0
1979 = 100	91.0	86.6	105.9	115.1	120.6	130.2
Dollar exports						
% growth rate	101.7	105.8	96.4	101.5	104.7	110.8
1979 = 100	101.7	81.7	101.7	103.2	108.0	119.7
Rouble imports						
% growth rate	104.3	92.1	105.7	106.4	104.3	101.8
1979 = 100	104.3	89.2	102.4	109.0	113.7	115.7
Dollar imports						
% growth rate	92.6	78.7	110.5	103.2	104.7	116.9
1979 = 100	92.6	50.4	67.6	69.8	73.1	85.4

Source: Statistical Yearbook of Foreign Trade 1987, 1988; GUS, Warsaw, 1988 and 1989

almost 50% over 1978–82. It is worth stressing that imports from industrialized countries started to fall even in 1977: in 1982 their volume was 60% below the 1976 level.

Owing to strong administrative restrictions aimed at curtailing imports from industrialized countries and a much smaller decline in exports, Poland managed to convert long-standing and regular hard currency deficits into a surplus (amounting to $1,433 mn fob) in 1982. This was possible partly thanks to a deficit in trade with payment area II of R 578 mn in the same year.

A marked import restructuring took place in 1979–80 when imports of capital and consumer goods were replaced by supplies of raw materials, components, parts and other intermediates. This provided Polish industry with essential productive inputs and allowed a recovery to start in the second half of 1982. Since 1982, after martial law was introduced and Western sanctions imposed, the end-use restructuring of imports was also accompanied by a geographical reorientation of Polish trade. It became a key policy objective to switch a substantial part of trade flows towards socialist countries, especially the Soviet Union. The idea was to make the Polish economy less dependent on Western countries. The feasibility of this trade reorientation was strongly questioned by many experts who argued that for technological reasons the substitutability of one set of imports for another would be low.[1] Also, it did not seem possible that hard-currency imports of raw materials for agricultural produce and food sector imports, worth $2 bn annually, could be compensated for by the increase of non-convertible currency imports. Thus, despite official policy declarations, it always seemed unlikely that the geographical restructuring of Polish trade flows would be able to overcome the trade barrier and to usher in any long-term economic recovery.

After 1982 foreign trade grew rapidly and faster than the economy as a whole but Poland's world trade share continued to fall. During 1983–8 GMP rose by 28.8% while the volume of exports grew by 47% and imports by 46.9%. Exports to centrally-planned economies (trading area I) increased by 50.3% and to trading area II countries by 46.5% while imports grew by 29.7% and 69.4% respectively. As a result, after a sharp decline during 1982–6, the share of market-economy countries, and particularly industrialized ones, in Polish trade turnover displayed a certain improvement over the 1986–8 period. In volume terms (constant 1984 prices) the share of Western economies in Polish imports was 42.2% in 1981, then fell to its lowest level of 29.7% in 1986 and after two years of fast expansion it increased again to 36.5%. In current prices the improvement was even greater: from 37.2% in 1981 through 32.2% in 1985 to reach 45.9% in 1988. It needs to be remembered however that there was a much faster devaluation of the złoty against the dollar than against the Rouble. Poland's main trade partners in 1988 (data in parentheses refer to shares in total imports and exports respectively) were: the Soviet Union (23.3% and 24.5%), West Germany (13.3% and 12.4%), Czechoslovakia (6.4% and 6.0%), GDR (5.0% and 4.4%), UK (3.3% and 5.0%), Austria (4.4% and 3.1%), Switzerland (4.5% and 2.6%) and Yugoslavia (3.3% and 2.7%).

Export growth varied from one year to another displaying significant annual oscillations. After three years of relatively high growth rates (8.7% to 10.3% in 1982–4), in the following three-year period (1985–7) export growth slowed considerably (see Table 13.2). In 1988 an acceleration took place but – according to initial estimates for 1989 – this proved a temporary phenomenon: in constant prices exports were marginally below the 1988 level. Annual variations were deeper in the case of hard currency exports: the two extremes were 1985 when exports dropped by 3.6% and 1983 when an increase of 14.9% was recorded.

Developments in the case of imports were slightly different. The fluctuations were smaller if compared to exports, in trade with both centrally-planned economies and market-economy countries.

Over the 1981–6 period the Rouble area trade balance was in deficit. Its largest level recorded in 1981 (R −1,611 mn) was reduced to R −501 million in 1986 and thereafter a surplus appeared. The trade deficit *vis-à-vis* centrally-planned economies was financed predominantly through loans granted by the Soviet Union. As a result, by end 1989, Poland's foreign debt with respect to socialist countries was estimated at R 6.4 bn.

The balance of trade with the hard-currency area has been completely turned around with surpluses since 1982. However, performance in this field deteriorated after 1984 (during 1982–4 hard currency trade surpluses amounted to $1.4 bn to $1.5 bn) in view of the limited ability to reduce further the level of imports and owing to constraints on expanding mineral exports, especially coal. A temporary improvement took place in 1987 and resulted from the increase in

Table 13.4 Foreign trade balance with each trading area 1981–8 (exports & imports fob)

	1981	1982	1983	1984	1985	1986	1987	1988	1989*
Rouble area (R mn)									
Imports	7265	7404	8270	9293	10044	10830	10935	10819	10071
Exports	5772	6826	7656	8625	9329	10329	10950	11938	12145
Balance	–1493	–578	–614	–668	–715	–501	15	1119	2074
Dollar area ($ mn)									
Imports	5868	4309	4451	4808	5077	5437	5844	7302	7714
Exports	5772	5742	5890	6339	6137	6510	7079	8311	8457
Balance	–96	1433	1439	1531	1060	1073	1235	1009	743

* preliminary figures.
Source: Rocznik Statystyczny, various years and *Rzeczpospolita*, 1, February 1990.

exports of manufactured goods. In 1988, in spite of a substantial growth of exports, the trade balance in convertible currencies slipped down due to an import surge. This downward trend continued in 1989. According to preliminary estimates the hard currency trade surplus did not exceed $742 mn, 73% of 1988 level. It is worth adding that the dollar trade surpluses achieved during the second half of the 1980s were highly unsatisfactory and much below planned targets. The five-year plan for 1986–90 anticipated that the trade surplus would steadily grow each year to reach $2.0 bn to $2.2 bn by 1990.

During the 1980s certain changes in the commodity composition of Polish exports, especially towards market-economy countries, took place. Nevertheless, primary product and semi-processed goods still dominated the commodity cross-section of exports. A different picture prevailed in Poland's exports to centrally-planned economies where electro-engineering and chemical industries played a prominent role.

During the first post-crisis years (1983–4) the growth of export volume to the convertible-currency area was mainly of products with a low level of processing: no fundamental change in the commodity structure of Polish exports took place. The growth of raw materials exports to the West resulted from the low level of manufacturing output and the lack of demand for local raw materials and fuels. In 1985, the volume of exports to industrialized countries fell. This was particularly true for coal, metallurgical, mineral and electro-engineering products. Low quality was the chief reason for falling sales of Polish products in the West. The 'extensive' nature of export expansion to market-economy countries in 1983–4 made it virtually impossible to increase exports further. Several barriers were soon encountered in Western markets, the most important of which was the limited demand for raw materials and fuels – attempts to expand their exports further led simply to the decline of unit prices.

Table 13.5 Commodity structure of exports 1985–8 (constant prices of 1984)

Product group	1985		1987		1988	
	I	II	I	II	I	II
Fuel and power	9.9	20.9	8.4	16.7	9.2	13.8
Manufacturing:						
Metallurgy	5.9	12.6	5.7	10.9	4.6	12.2
Electro-engineering	57.5	18.0	57.5	21.8	58.3	23.0
Chemicals	9.4	10.5	10.0	11.3	10.1	11.4
Wood and paper	0.9	3.4	0.9	4.1	0.9	4.4
Light industry	5.5	6.5	5.5	7.8	4.9	8.1
Food processing	2.2	12.8	2.4	13.9	2.1	12.9
Construction	4.9	5.8	5.7	4.0	6.4	3.7
Agricultural products	2.1	5.7	2.2	6.4	2.0	6.5

I – non-convertible currencies; II – convertible currencies.
Source: Rocznik Statystyczny, various years.

From 1986 a certain improvement in the commodity composition of Polish exports to the hard-currency area took place. In 1988 the share of manufacturing products, in particular from electro-engineering and chemical industries, rose significantly though it should be noticed that the starting point was rather low. It is also worth noting that the shares of processed goods in Polish exports to industrialized Western countries are by several percentage points lower than the general figure for trading area II (encompassing also developing countries and hard-currency trade with centrally-planned economies). The commodity structure of Polish exports to socialist countries (payment area I) looks more favourable. Manufactures and processed goods, such as machinery and equipment, merchant vessels and other transport vehicles, chemicals, durable consumer goods and textiles play a prominent role. At the same time the share of primary commodities, such as fuel and power, metallurgy products, foodstuffs and agricultural products, is relatively low and has tended to decline. The high share of processed goods in exports to trading area I results to some extent from lower quality requirements in COMECON countries. It is to be expected, even in the near future, however, that quality and technology standards will also rise within this region.

A more favourable commodity structure of exports to the Rouble area countries has not been reflected in terms of trade (see Table 13.6). The Polish disadvantage here has stemmed from high prices of crude oil and natural gas, imported from the Soviet Union, with prices set according to a five-year moving average of world prices. But from 1987 oil and gas prices have fallen with a

Table 13.6 Terms of trade 1980–8

	1980	1981	1982	1983	1984	1985	1986	1987	1988	1989*
Rouble area										
previous year = 100	98.4	96.8	95.9	96.7	97.8	99.0	100.6	104.6	103.9	103.7
1978 = 100	95.8	92.6	88.8	85.9	84.0	83.2	83.7	87.7	91.0	94.4
$ area										
previous year = 100	100.1	99.1	102.4	94.3	98.6	105.2	101.4	102.2	100.9	101.3
1978 = 100	98.9	98.0	100.4	94.7	93.4	98.3	99.7	101.9	102.8	104.1

Source: Statistical Yearbook of Foreign Trade 1986, GUS, Warsaw, 1986; GUS *Rocznik Statystyczny 1987* and *1989*, Warsaw, 1987, 1989.
* Initial estimates, *Rzeczpospolita*, 1 February 1990.

slight terms-of-trade improvement. With respect to the hard-currency area the terms of trade remained rather neutral during the crisis period in 1979–82 but a deterioration was recorded in 1983–4, when coal and other mineral exports were growing and world market prices were falling. Since 1985, however, the terms of trade *vis-à-vis* this area have modestly improved.

As far as the commodity composition of imports, as seen from end-use, is concerned two characteristic features during the 1980s emerge. First, the dramatic cuts in overall imports at the turn of 1970s and 1980s, particularly from Western countries, were partly compensated for by a substantial increase of the share of so-called supply imports, that is inputs for current production (raw materials, components and parts). The relative stability of supply imports was one of the most essential factors contributing to the economic recovery in Poland from the second half of 1982. From 1985 the share of supply imports tended to decline in favour of consumer goods imports (see Table 13.7). Second, even when supply imports' share started to fall capital goods imports share

Table 13.7 End-use composition of imports 1980–8 (%)

	1980	1985	1986	1987	1988
Total	100.0	100.0	100.0	100.0	100.0
of which					
Supply imports	73.1	68.5	66.8	67.4	65.9
Investment imports	13.8	10.0	11.1	11.8	11.9
Consumer imports	7.6	10.2	11.7	10.4	12.7

Source: Rocznik Statystyczny 1989.

remained low. Holding investment goods imports at this very low level jeopardized Poland's long-term development prospects.

While analyzing the role foreign trade played in the development of the Polish economy in the 1980s one more important inter-relationship comes to light. This was the low, and mainly declining, import elasticity of GMP (especially after 1983). In view of the idle capacities in Polish industry this phenomenon ought to be seen in a negative light.

3. Future prospects for Polish foreign trade

Any attempt to suggest how trade (or any other area for that matter) may develop both in the near and more distant future is extremely difficult and risky. This is because:

– in early 1990, Poland was in an economic transition which was likely to reach a peak of intensity in the first quarter of the year. However, the radical programme which was launched on 1 January 1990 could not alter short-run 'facts of life'. Most important here was the 'system vacuum': the old, command-type economic mechanism had ceased to function while the market mechanism had not yet been properly established.

– shifts in the political and social situation, which are of fundamental significance for the success or failure of the Balcerowicz programme (and vice versa), are hard to predict. Of primary importance here will be the scale and duration of social support for the government and endurance of the economic hardships following the austerity programme.

– there are no historical precedents for such a radical and time-compressed systemic transformation upon which to draw.

Paradoxically, it is relatively easier to say something about likely longer-run trade developments. A new economic system based on the market, coupled with efficiency-oriented restructuring, should open the economy and expand its foreign trade operations. It should also entail a more rational international specialization and establish new patterns of foreign trade, taking proper account of existing factor proportions and comparative advantage. But for this to happen the Balcerowicz programme must succeed. It is a prerequisite for the successful establishment of a market-based economic mechanism in Poland that inflation is brought under control.

As far as short-term developments in foreign trade are concerned, all predictions are burdened with high risk and uncertainty. Therefore it seems reasonable to sketch in the broadest terms only what may be the most likely impact on foreign trade of the Balcerowicz programme.

The government programme hoped that 1990 would consist of two quite different sub-periods: the first (January–June) would be devoted to overcoming inflation and would impose recession and severe hardships; the second (July–December) would bring some easing of the social and economic situation and the start of economic recovery. The programme envisaged that strong anti-inflationary measures would produce a decline in manufacturing output of 5% and in GMP of up to 3% in 1990. This would, it was thought, inevitably reduce trade activity, at least in the first half of the year, which would mean a continuation of the downward trend in trade that emerged in the last quarter of 1989.

Some economists, however, suggested that the slump in output could be far greater and reach 20% in the year, and even more during the first half of 1990. Certainly enterprises faced an immensely difficult situation in 1990. Production costs (energy, fuels, imports) grew dramatically as did the tax burden, (particularly the tax on revalued assets) and credit costs (positive interest rates). This happened alongside removal of tax reliefs, export and investment allowances. Undoubtedly many industries will meet serious problems in maintaining sales (the 'demand barrier', perhaps also competition from imported goods). As a result, many firms may go bankrupt. If this number is greater than expected, the output decline will deepen and further disrupt the sub-contracting network, accelerating the downward spiral whose eventual scale remains unpredictable.

The government expected that from the second half of 1990, provided the anti-inflationary measures proved successful, the first symptoms of recovery would appear: the monthly inflation rate should be down to several per cent, consumer and supply markets will be brought into equilibrium, speculation will be halted, productivity of labour increased, Poland will be closer to the world market, the złoty will exclusively perform its monetary functions as the only currency in Poland, the attractiveness of savings should be restored (positive real interest rate on deposits) and finally, economic recovery coupled wth stability, diminishing tax burdens, the inflow of foreign capital and switching a part of productive assets to more efficient uses should begin. All this is obviously possible: the question remains however, what is its probability?

The Balcerowicz programme faces considerable dangers. It would be enough for just one or two links to break: the government could fail to halt wage increases, the banks could fail to sustain złoty convertibility, the exchange rate could come under pressure, the output decline could be too deep and Western aid too little.

It is clear that under the optimistic scenario both exports and imports should start growing from the second half of 1990 while under the pessimistic one the reverse happens, additionally fuelling economic breakdown. Apart from this very general view the final outcome in the field of foreign trade will heavily depend on what happens as a result of the use of different economic tools aimed at stifling inflation, such as the exchange rate, tax policy, monetary and credit policies.

3.1. Exchange rate

The 'internal' złoty convertibility which was introduced on 1 January 1990, combined with its dramatic devaluati n (if compared to mid-November 1989 it was devalued by over 200% to zł 9,500 per dollar) will inevitably affect the propensity to export and import. The 1 January rate should strongly encourage exports although other components of the stabilization programme may neutralize or even cancel this expansive impact. The other elements include a very restrictive tax policy and deflationary credit and monetary targets.

Simultaneously the new exchange rate will in principle curb firms' propensity to import, though in the existing environment (strong monopolistic structures, lack of domestic competition) enterprises are able in the short run to bear much higher import costs and to pass them on in the prices charged to the customers.

The 1 January 1990 exchange rate should also spur the inflow of foreign direct investment and, as a consequence, produce trade creation and diversion effects (new exports and imports, changes in their commodity structure). On the other hand some other factors (to be discussed later) may also discourage investors from coming to Poland.

3.2. Tax policy

This was designed predominantly as a tool to generate increased revenues for the state budget to liquidate the huge deficit inherited from 1989. The main components of tax policy in 1990 were: uniformity of tax rules for all sectors (that is no longer any special privileges for simply being a state sector economic organization), a huge increase in firms' tax burdens (including a Treasury dividend paid on revalued – by a factor of eleven – fixed assets), the removal of all individual and/or discretionary tax reliefs and exemptions as well as sharpening tax sanctions for excessive wage increases. In the short run this policy may adversely affect the volume of output and hence discourage producers from expanding their exports, even if the exchange rate provides strong incentives to do so. This negative trend may be strengthened by two factors:

– the liquidation of general tax reliefs on exports existing under the previous tax regime;

– the relative worsening of conditions for foreign investors (the withdrawal of corporate tax reliefs on exports which under the pre 1 January 1990 system allowed the profits tax burden to be reduced to a minimum 10% and gave investors the right to retain 85% of hard currency export earnings).

On the other hand, the exclusion of joint ventures from the general 'tax penalties' on excessive wage increases should encourage foreign investors to expand output and exports.

3.3. Monetary and credit policy

The policy goals of the stabilization programme include, among other things, positive real interest rates on loans extended to enterprises and hard budget constraints in terms of tight monetary targets and strict central bank control over the money supply. The immediate outcome of this policy, apart from slowing down inflation, could easily be an excessive economic recession and concomitant slump in exports and imports. On the other hand, export opportunities may positively contribute to softening sales troubles on the domestic market as households' real incomes fall by 25–30% as envisaged in the Balcerowicz programme. Moreover, excessive prices on domestic products may encourage the inflow of competitive imported goods and – in the longer term – foreign direct investment.

3.4. Custom duties

Since 1 January 1990 all imported items are subject to generalized custom duties and turnover tax, and uniform rules are being applied to all sectors of the economy. These measures, combined with the new exchange rate policy, will probably additionally discourage imports (especially in case of consumer goods where higher custom and tax rates also applied) and slow down the process of using foreign competition as a means of countervailing domestic monopolistic practices. The propensity and ability of Polish firms to import will also be adversely affected by tight monetary and credit policy which will create liquidity problems and may lead firms to sell stocks of foreign exchange from ROD accounts[2] simply to increase liquidity.

In conclusion, even if the stabilization programme brings the economy to a safe haven, more fundamental qualitative and structural adjustments to foreign trade patterns will require a longer period. They will also depend on the success of the second stage of the Balcerowicz programme, that is, the successful setting up of a Western-style market economy in Poland.

Notes

1. See for example, *Polish Economy in the External Environment in the 1980s*, World Economy Research Institute, Central School of Planning and Statistics, Warsaw, 1988, and *Raport o sytuacji i perspektywach gospodarczych Polski w latach 1987–1996* (Report on the economic situation and perspectives in Poland in 1987–1996), ed. J. Pawilno-Pacewicz, Warsaw, 1987.
2. ROD accounts are firms' own foreign exchange accounts. These were introduced in the reforms of the 1980s and allowed exporters a proportion of foreign exchange earnings for own use. Under the post January 1990 set-up of 'internal' złoty convertibility the ROD accounts are being phased out. In the new system exporters must sell all foreign exchange earnings to the state but may then purchase as much as is needed for imports and investment from the banks. See also Chapter 3 by Dariusz Rosati for more background on the ROD scheme.

♦ INDEX ♦

Agriculture 56–62
   Investments in 1980s 80
   Private 57
Aid
   International to fight pollution 42–3, 133
American Bank in Poland 97–8
Ascherson, Neal 1

Balcerowicz
   Impact of 'Mark 1' policies 2, 92
   and trade 143–4
Banking
   monobank system 95–6
Balchatow lignite mine 46
Bush, President 43

Cambridge equation 85
Catholic
   Association 12, 13
   Church 5, 12, 13
Coal output 44, 45
Coal lobby 53
Comecon 136, 141
Commercialization of enterprises 113
   see also privatization
Convertibility
   Internal of złoty 27, 29, 92, 144–5
   see also złoty stabilisation fund
Communist Party (PUWP/PZPR) 9, 11
   Central Committee 12
   Politburo 12
   Splits in Party 17
Crop production 60

Debt
   Creditor structure 129
   Non-official 127–8
   Official 126–7
   Rescheduling 126–7
Disequilibrium 84
Dollarization of economy 104

Ecodevelopment 39
Ecologically threatened areas 33, 40
Economic reforms 1981–2 21
   Banking reform 95–7
   Planning under 22
   Prices 22, 26, 53, 88–9
   Second stage of 26
Election, June 1989 15
Energy supply 44–8
   Prices 53
Exchange rate policy 144–5
   see also convertibility
Export retention quotas 23, 146

Farms
   Private 57, 110
Foreign trade organisations (FTOs) 136
Front of National Unity 12
Fuel
   and energy balance 1975–90 45
   and energy investment in 1980s 80–1
   Losses due to fuel and energy efficiency 50

Gierek-Jaroszewicz programme 21
Green Party 38

Housing
  Construction 65
  Impact of Mazowiecki government on 69
  Investment in 1980s 80
  Policy 63–5

IMF 30, 31, 97, 99, 133
  1981 application 118
  Backing for new policies in 1990 132
  see also złoty stabilisation fund
Inflation in 1990 30, 84–94
Investments abandoned in early 1980s 73, 81

Jaruzelski, Wojciech 15
  Presidency 16
  and Messner government 25

Katowice banking school 105
Know-how fund 105
Kornai 27, 84
Kraków 43
Kuczyński, Waldemar 117

Martial law 15, 23
  and debt 119, 126, 127
  and economic policy 120
  and trade reorientation 138
Mazowiecki, Tadeusz 1, 2, 16
  and foreign creditors 132
  economic programme 28–30
  popular support 31
Monoparty system 2
Mikołajczyk 16

National Bank of Poland 27, 95–8
Nomenklatura 16
Nuclear power see Żarnowiec 47

Oil supply 47
OPZZ 15, 18

Paris Club 119, 126
Parliament (Sejm)
  Division of seats 12, 15
Philips, A.W. 86
Pollution in Silesia 33, 46
Prices
  Administrative (urzedowe) 22, 88–9
  Contract (umowne) 26, 88–9
  Regulated (regulowane) 22, 88–9
  Price shock 1982 103–4
Private sector 107
  in agriculture 110
Privatization
  and environment 41
  Programme 112, 113
PRON 15

Rakowski 27
Rescheduling see debt
Round table 1, 9, 15, 70
Rychard, Andrzej 7

Social dimorphism 7
Solidarity 8, 14, 15
  Future scenarios 18
  Internal splits 9, 16
Soviet Union
  and debt discussions 128, 132
  and oil supply 47
  and perestroika 17
Subsidies 27

Trade balances 140
  Commodity structure 141

Wałęsa, L 16
Workers' Defence Committee 14
World Bank
  Lending 133
  Study on Poland 52

Żarnowiec 47
Złoty stabilisation fund 30, 92